Let It Begin with Me

Spurgeon on Revival

Edited by Robert Backhouse

SERVANT PUBLICATIONS
ANN ARBOR, MICHIGAN

Vine Books is an imprint of Servant Publications especially designed to serve
evangelical Christians.

Unless otherwise indicated, biblical quotations are from the Authorized Version
(King James Version), Crown copyright.

Published by Servant Publications
P.O. Box 8617
Ann Arbor, Michigan 48107

Cover design: Brian Fowler, DesignTeam, Grand Rapids, Michigan

97 98 99 00 01 10 9 8 7 6 5 4 3 2 1

Printed in the United States of America
ISBN 1-56955-015-8

Library of Congress Cataloging-in-Publication Data

Spurgeon, C. H. (Charles Haddon), 1834-1892
[Spurgeon on revival]
Let it begin with me : Spurgeon on revival / edited by Robert Backhouse.
    p.   cm.
Originally published: Spurgeon on revival. Eastbourne, East Sussex, England :
Kingsway Publications, 1996.
Includes bibliographical references.
ISBN 1-56955-015-8
1. Church renewal—Sermons.   2. Evangelistic work—Sermons.   3. Baptists—
Sermons.   4. Sermons, English.   I. Backhouse, Robert.   II. Title.
BV3797.S645   1997
252'3—dc21
                                                              97-31
                                                               CIP

Wilt thou not revive us again:
that thy people may rejoice in thee?

———

PSALMS 85:6

Contents

Introduction

This book sets out to answer two questions: "What is revival?" and "What is the route to revival?"

What is revival? Good definitions of revival are hard to come by. Dr. J. I. Packer has written that "revival, as Protestant theology has used the word for 250 years, means God's quickening visitation of his people, touching their hearts and deepening his work of grace in their lives."[1]

This book gives answers to the question "What is revival?" by returning to the pages of the Bible in the company of the great nineteenth-century British Baptist preacher, C. H. Spurgeon. Spurgeon, the most popular preacher of his day, with more than 100 million copies of his sermons in print some years after his death, charts the path to revival, both for the individual and for a church fellowship.

Spurgeon found no contradiction in praying for revival and in working for it tirelessly. Through his faithful preaching from God's word in the six-thousand-seat Metropolitan Tabernacle, London, Spurgeon was used by God to bring fourteen thousand new members to the congregation, resulting in many churches being "planted" in different parts of London. Each Sunday morning, as Spurgeon climbed up the steps of his pulpit, he prayed under his breath, "I believe in the Holy Spirit. I believe in the Holy Spirit. I believe in the Holy Spirit." Spurgeon was a living monument to the work of God's revival in the human heart.

In revival God visits his people, making his presence known and revealing himself as the holy God. This then throws human sin into stark relief. During times of revival there is increased awareness of the sinfulness of sin, and people willingly accept that they are hell-deserving sinners. The extract from Spurgeon's *Treasury of the New Testament* on Acts 2:36-37 emphasizes this essential aspect of true revival. For Spurgeon, revival was an impossibility if members of his congregation were "grieving the Holy Spirit." So Spurgeon's sermon on Ephesians 4:30—"Do not grieve the Holy Spirit of God"—showed his hearers how they were to please God in times of revival.

In revival people are overcome and overwhelmed by God's love. Men, women, and children are immersed in God's forgiveness and redemption, focused most clearly on the cross of our Lord. There are always two consequences of genuine revival. First, Satan does not take a back seat. There are real and powerful satanic attacks on people involved in the revival. Second, God's work seems to take on a special urgency, and this is pinpointed in Spurgeon's sermon concerning mission and revival, based on John 16:8-11. Spurgeon labors the point repeatedly that "the Holy Spirit makes the world know that Christ is righteous." "Now listen to the Spirit of God. The Spirit came into the world to make everyone know that Jesus is the Christ, and he attested that fact by miracles that could not be questioned, miracles without number."

Spurgeon never prescribes a heavenly remedy before diagnosing the spiritual ailment. His analysis of the spiritual state of individuals and churches is always radical, as is seen in this comment:

Withering is a most necessary experience, and just now needs to be greatly insisted on. Today we have so many built up who were never pulled down; so many filled who were never emptied; so many exalted who were never humbled; that I more earnestly remind you that the Holy Spirit must convince us of sin, or we cannot be saved.

Some people find it difficult to distinguish between conversion and revival, for many, and sometimes all, of these experiences are felt by people at their conversion. So, it is asked, how can such people need any kind of reviving? Are they not already spiritually alive with God's Spirit? This question is touched on in the last chapter of this book. Here Spurgeon expounds Revelation 2:4-7, where the need to return to our first love of the Lord Jesus Christ is heavily underlined. Spurgeon concludes this sermon with these words:

We will know as we are known when we love as we are loved. We will live the life of God when we are wholly taken up with the love of God. The love of Jesus answered by our love for Jesus makes the sweetest music the heart can know. No joy on earth is equal to this bliss of being all taken up with love for Christ. Heaven on earth is abounding love towards Jesus.

Spurgeon pleaded with his congregation, to whom he had been preaching for thirty-three years, that both they and he should take action when they lost their first love of Jesus. He said: "As a church we must love Jesus, or else we have lost our reason for existence." This view of revival shows that revival should be a constant experience rather than just a flash in the pan, for Christians are running a marathon, not making a sixty-meter dash. Paul once said to some of his Christian friends, "You were running a good race," and he added an embarrassing question: "Who cut in on you and kept you from obeying the truth?" (Gal 5:7). Revival is a realistic possibility, indeed a necessity, for everyone who has slowed down in the Christian race.

True revival is God's will for us, though it is a mistake to think—as some Christians claim—that if special spiritual formulas are worked out, and if certain spiritual laws are followed, then God will inevitably pour out dramatic blessings in the form of revival. One way to escape from misusing the Bible and merely going to it for "proof texts" is to remember that a "text out of context is a pretext." In other words, we need to study the Bible's teaching on revival in the context in which the Bible places revival. In these edited sermons of Spurgeon we discover that this so-called "uneducated" country preacher is a past master at expounding the verses which come before and after specific verses about revival. He does not take isolated "golden texts" on revival and chop them off from their context. By carefully noting the context in which God's teaching about revival is revealed to us in the pages of the Bible, our understanding and experience of revival are greatly deepened and broadened.

Robert Backhouse
Norfolk, 1995

Note

1. S. B. Ferguson and D. F. Wright (eds), *New Dictionary of Theology* (IVP, 1973), 588.

PART 1

===

The Treasury of David
Psalms of Revival

CHAPTER ONE

Pining for God's Presence
Psalms 42 and 43

PSALM 42

Verse 1. "As the hart panteth after the water brooks, so panteth my soul after thee, O God." As the hunted hart instinctively seeks the river to bathe its smoking flanks and to escape the dogs, so my weary, persecuted soul pants after the Lord my God. Debarred from public worship, David was heartsick. Ease he did not seek, honor he did not covet, but the enjoyment of communion with God was an urgent and absolute necessity, like water to a stag. Have you personally felt the same? The next best thing to living in the light of the Lord's love is to be unhappy till we have it, and to pant hourly after it. Thirst is a perpetual appetite. When it is as natural for us to long after God as for an animal to thirst, it is well with our souls, however painful our feelings. The eagerness of our desires may be pleaded with God, and the more so because there are special promises for the importunate and fervent.

Verse 2. "My soul": all my nature, my inmost self. "Thirsteth": hunger you can palliate, but thirst is awful, insatiable, deadly.

"For God": not merely for the temple and the ordinances, but for fellowship with God himself. None but the spiritual can sympathize with this thirst.

"For the living God": because he lives, and gives the living water, therefore we with greater eagerness desire him.

"When shall I come and appear before God?" He who loves the Lord loves also the assemblies wherein his name is adored. Vain are all claims to religion where the outward means of grace have no attraction. David was never so much at home as in the house of the Lord; he was not content with private worship; he did not forsake the place where saints assemble, as the manner of some is. After God, his *Elohim* (his God to be worshiped, who had entered into covenant with him), he pined as the drooping flowers for the dew. If all our resortings to public worship were viewed as appearances before God, it would be a sure mark of grace to delight in them. Alas, how many appear before the minister, or their fellow-men, and think that enough! "To see the face of God" is a nearer translation of the Hebrew; but the two ideas may be combined—he would see his God and be seen by him; this is worth thirsting after!

Verse 3. "My tears have been my meat day and night." Salty meats, but healthful to the soul. Those who come to tears, plenteous tears, are in earnest indeed. There is a dry grief far more terrible than showery sorrows. David's tears, since they were shed because God was blasphemed, were "honorable dew," drops of holy water, such as Jehovah puts in his bottle.

"While they continually say unto me, Where is thy God?"

Cruel taunts come naturally from cowardly minds. Surely they might have left the mourner alone; he could weep no more than he did—it was a supererogation of malice to pump more tears from a heart which already overflowed. Note how incessant was the jeer, and how artfully they framed it! It cut the good man to the bone to have the faithfulness of his God impugned. The wicked know that our worst misfortune would be to lose God's favor; hence their diabolical malice leads them to declare that such is the case. Glory be to God, they lie in their throats, for our God is in the heavens, and in the furnace too, succoring his people.

Verse 4. "When I remember these things, I pour out my soul in me." When he harped upon his woes his heart melted into water and was poured out upon itself. God hidden, and foes raging, a pair of evils enough to bring down the stoutest heart! Yet why let reflections so gloomy engross us, since the result is of no value: merely to turn the soul on itself, to empty it from itself into itself is useless; how much better to pour out the heart before the Lord! The prisoner's treadwheel might sooner land him in the skies than mere inward questioning raise us nearer to consolation.

"For I had gone with the multitude, I went with them to the house of God." Painful reflections were awakened by the memory of past joys; he had mingled in the pious throng, their numbers had hoped to give him exhilaration and to awaken holy delight, their company had been a charm to him as with them he ascended the hill of Zion. With frequent strains of song, he and the people of Jehovah had marched in reverent ranks up to the shrine of sacrifice, the dear abode of peace and holiness. Far away from such goodly company the holy man pictures the sacred scene and dwells upon the details of the pious march.

"With the voice of joy and praise, with a multitude that kept holyday." Perhaps he alludes to the removal of the ark and to the glorious gatherings of the tribes on that grand national holy day and holiday. How changed his present place! For Zion, a wilderness; for the priests in white linen, soldiers in garments of war; for the song, the sneer of blasphemy; for the festivity, lamentation; for joy in the Lord, a mournful dirge over his absence. David appears to have had a peculiarly tender remembrance of the *singing* of the pilgrims, and assuredly it is the most delightful part of worship and that which comes nearest to the adoration of heaven. What a degradation to supplant the intelligent song of the whole congregation by the theatrical prettinesses of a quartet, the refined niceties of a choir, or inanimate bellows and pipes! We might as well pray by machinery as praise by it.

Verse 5. "Why art thou cast down, O my soul?" As though he were two men, the psalmist talks to himself. These present troubles, are they to last forever? The rejoicings of my foes, are they more than empty talk? My absence from the solemn feasts, is that a perpetual exile? Why this deep depression? To search out the causes of our sorrow is often the best surgery for grief. Self-ignorance is not bliss; in this case it is misery. The mist of ignorance magnifies the causes of our alarm; a clearer view will make monsters dwindle into trifles.

"Why art thou disquieted in me?" Why is my quiet gone? If I cannot keep a public Sabbath, yet wherefore do I deny my soul her indoor Sabbath? Why am I agitated like a troubled sea, and why do my thoughts make a noise like a tumultuous multitude? The causes are not enough to justify such utter yielding to despondency. Up, my heart! Your castings down will turn to liftings up, and your disquietudes to calm.

"Hope thou in God." If every evil is let loose from Pandora's box, yet is there hope at the bottom. God is unchangeable, and therefore his grace is the ground for unshaken hope. If everything be dark, yet the day will come, and meanwhile hope carries stars in her eyes; her lamps are not dependent upon oil from without, her light is fed by secret visitations of God, which sustain the spirit.

"For I shall yet praise him for the help of his countenance." Salvations come from the propitious face of God, and he will yet lift up his countenance upon us. Note well that the main hope and chief desire of David rest in the smile of God. This verse, like the singing of Paul and Silas, looses chains and shakes prison walls. He who can use such heroic language in his gloomy hours will surely conquer.

Verse 6. "O my God, my soul is cast down within me." Perhaps the spasm of despondency returned. With God the song begins the second time more nearly than the first. The singer was also a little more tranquil. Outward expression of desire was gone; there was no visible panting; the sorrow was now all restrained within doors. Within or upon himself he was cast down; it may well be so while our thoughts look more within than upward. If self were to furnish comfort, we should have but poor provender. There is no solid foundation for comfort in such fickle frames as our heart is subject to. It is well to tell the Lord how we feel, and the more plain the confession the better.

"Therefore will I remember thee": blessed downcasting

which drives us to so sure a rock of refuge as thee, O Lord!

"From the hill Mizar": he recalls his seasons of choice communion by the river and among the hills, and especially that dearest hour upon the little hill where love spoke her sweetest language and revealed her nearest fellowship. It is great wisdom to store up in memory our choice occasions of converse with heaven; we may want them another day, when the Lord is slow in bringing back his banished ones, and our soul is aching with fear. Or does David mean that even where he was he would think of his God; does he declare that, forgetful of time and place, he would count Hermon as holy as Zion, and even Mizar, that insignificant rising ground, as glorious as the mountains which are round about Jerusalem?

Verse 7. "Deep calleth unto deep at the noise of thy waterspouts." Thy severe dealings with me seem to excite all creation to attack me; heaven, and earth, and hell call to each other, stirring each other up in dreadful conspiracy against my peace. As in a waterspout, the deeps above and below clasp hands, so it seemed to David that heaven and earth united to create a tempest around him. His woes were incessant and overwhelming. His soul seemed drowned as in a universal deluge of trouble, over whose waves the providence of the Lord moved as a watery pillar, in dreadful majesty inspiring the utmost terror. As for the afflicted one, he was like a mariner floating on a mast, almost every moment submerged.

"All thy waves and thy billows are gone over me." David thought that every trouble in the world had met in him, but he exaggerated, for "all" the breaking waves of Jehovah have passed over none but the Lord Jesus. Yet what a plight to be in! Most of the heirs of heaven have experienced the like. This is a deep experience unknown to babes in grace, but common enough to such as do business on great waters of affliction: to such it is some comfort to remember that the waves and billows are the Lord's—"*thy* waves and *thy* billows"—they are all sent and directed by him, and achieve his purposes.

Verse 8. "Yet the LORD will command his lovingkindness in the daytime": lovingkindness is a noble life-belt in a rough sea. The day may darken into a strange and untimely midnight, but the love of God ordained of old to be the portion of the elect shall be by sovereign grace meted out to them. No day shall ever dawn on an heir of grace and find him altogether forsaken of his Lord; the Lord reigns, and as a sovereign he will with authority command mercy to be reserved for his chosen.

"And in the night": both divisions of the day will be illuminated with special love, and no stress or trial will prevent it. Our God is God of the nights as well as the days.

"His song shall be with me": songs of praise for blessings received will cheer the gloom of the night. The belief that we shall yet glorify the Lord for mercy given in extremity is a delightful stay to the soul.

"And my prayer unto the God of my life": prayer is yoked with praise. The living God is the God of our life; from him we derive it, with him in prayer and praise we spend it, to him we devote it, in him we shall perfect it. To be assured that our sighs and songs will both have free access to our glorious Lord is to have reasons for hope in the most deplorable condition.

Verse 9. "I will say unto God my rock, Why hast thou forgotten me?" Faith is allowed to inquire of her God the causes of his displeasure, and she is even permitted to expostulate with him and remind him of his promises, and ask why apparently they are not fulfilled. If the Lord be indeed our refuge, when we find no refuge, it is time to be raising the question, "Why is this?" Yet we must not let go our hold; the Lord must be "my" rock still.

"Why go I mourning because of the oppression of the enemy?" Surely God can have no pleasure in seeing the faces of his servants stained and squalid with their tears; he can find no contentment in the harshness with which their foes assail them. How can the strong God, who is as firm and abiding as a rock, be also as hard and unmoved as a rock towards those who trust in him? Such inquiries humbly pressed often afford relief to the soul. To know the reason for sorrow is in part to know how to escape it, or at least to endure it. Lack of attentive consideration often makes adversity appear to be more mysterious and hopeless than it really is. It is a pitiable thing for anyone to have a limb amputated, but when we know that the operation was needed in order to save life, we are glad to hear that it has been successfully performed.

Verse 10. "As with a sword in my bones, mine enemies reproach me": cruel mockeries cut deeper than the flesh; they reach the soul. The tongue cuts to the bone, and its wounds are hard to cure.

"While they say daily unto me, Where is thy God?" This is the unkindest cut of all, reflecting as it does both upon the Lord's faithfulness and his servant's character. Such was the malice of David's foes that they repeated the cruel question "daily." Surely this was enough to madden him, and perhaps would have done so had he not resorted to prayer.

Verse 11. "Why art thou cast down, O my soul? and why art thou disquieted within me?" He finds after all no sufficient ground for being disquieted. Looked in the face, his fears were not so overwhelming as they seemed when shrouded in obscurity.

"Hope thou in God": let the anchor still keep its hold. God is faithful, God is love, there is room and reason for hope.

"Who is the health of my countenance, and my God": this is the same hopeful expression as that contained in verse 5, but the addition of "and my God" shows that the writer was growing in confidence, and was able defiantly to reply to the question, "Where is thy God?" Here he is, ready to deliver me. I am not ashamed to own him amid your sneers and taunts, for he will rescue me out of your hands. Thus faith closes the struggle, a victor in fact by anticipation, and in heart by firm reliance. The saddest countenance will yet be made to shine, if there be a taking of God at his word and an expectation of his salvation.

PSALM 43

Verse 1. "Judge me, O God": others are unable to understand my motives, and unwilling to give me a just verdict. My heart is clear as to its intent, and therefore I bring my case before thee, content that thou wilt impartially weigh my character, and right my wrongs. If thou wilt judge, thy acceptance of my conduct will be enough for me; I can laugh at human misrepresentation if my conscience knows that thou art on my side; thou art the only one I care for; and besides, thou wilt see practical justice done to thy slandered servant.

"And plead my cause against an ungodly nation": one such advocate as the Lord will more than suffice to answer a nation of brawling accusers. When people are ungodly, no wonder they are unjust; those who are not true to God himself cannot be expected to deal rightly with his people.

"O deliver me from the deceitful and unjust man": from such devils none can deliver us but God. His wisdom can outwit the craft of the vilest serpent, and his power can overmatch the most raging lion. If we try to fight them with our own weapons we shall suffer more serious injury from ourselves than from them. Vengeance belongeth not to us, but to our Lord. Turn to him in prayer, and ere long you will publish abroad the remembrance of his salvation.

Verse 2. "For": here is argument, which is the very sinew of prayer. If we reasoned more with the Lord we should have more victories in supplication.

"Thou art the God of my strength": all my strength belongs to thee. I will not, therefore, use it on my own behalf against my personal foes; I seek help from thee; I leave the task of combating my foes entirely in thy hands. Note the assurance of David: "thou art," not "I hope and trust so," but "I know it is so."

"Why dost thou cast me off?" There are many reasons why the Lord might cast us off, but no reason will prevail to make him do so. He has not cast off his people, though he for a while treats them as castoffs. It is well to inquire into dark providences, but we must inquire of God, not of our own fears. He who is the author of a mysterious trial can best expound it to us.

"Why go I mourning because of the oppression of the enemy?" Why do I wander hither and thither like a restless spirit? Why do I wear the weeds of sorrow on my body, and the lines of grief on my face? Oppression makes a wise man mad; why, Lord, am I called to endure so much of it for so long a time? Here again is a useful question, addressed to the right quarter. The answer will often be because we are saints, and must be made like our Head, and because such sorrow is chastening to the spirit, and yields fruit. We are not to cross-question the Lord in peevishness, but we may ask of him in humility; God help us to observe the distinction so as not to sin through stress of sorrow.

Verse 3. "O send out thy light and thy truth." The joy of thy presence and the faithfulness of thy heart—let both of these be manifest to me. Reveal my true character by thy light, and reward me according to thy truthful promise. As the sun darts out his beams, so does the Lord send out his favor and his faithfulness towards all his people, lighting up even our darkest surroundings with delightful splendor.

"Let them lead me": be these my star to guide me to my rest.

"Let them bring me unto thy holy hill, and to thy tabernacles": first in thy mercy bring me to thy earthly courts, and end my weary exile, and then in due time admit me to thy celestial palace above. We seek not light to sin by, nor truth to be exalted by it, but that they may become our practical guides to the nearest communion with God: only such light and truth as are sent us from God will do this; common light is not strong enough, nor will mere moral or physical truths assist to the holy hill; but the light of the Holy Spirit, and the truth as it is in Jesus, these are elevating, sanctifying, perfecting; and hence their virtue in leading us to the glorious presence of God. It is beautiful to observe how David's longing to be away from the oppression of man always leads him to sigh more intensely for communion with God.

Verse 4. "Then will I go unto the altar of God." If David might be permitted to return, it would not be his own house which would be his first resort, but the altar of God. With what exultation should believers draw near to Christ, who is the antitype of the altar!

"Unto God my exceeding joy": It was not the altar as such that the psalmist cared for, but fellowship with God himself. What are all the rites of worship unless the Lord be in them? God is not David's "joy" alone, but his "exceeding" joy; not the fountain of joy, the giver of joy, or the maintainer of joy, but that joy itself. The margin has "the gladness of joy," that is, the soul, the essence of my joy. To draw near to God, who is such a joy to us, may well be the object of our hungering and thirsting.

"Yea, upon the harp will I praise thee": when God fills us with joy we ought ever to pour it out at his feet in praise, and all the skill and talent we have should be laid under contribution to increase the divine revenue of glory.

"O God, my God": how he dwells upon the name which he loves so well! To have God in possession, and to know it by faith, is the heart's heaven.

Verse 5. "Why art thou cast down, O my soul?" If God be thine, why this dejection?

"And why art thou disquieted within me?" Wherefore indulge unreasonable sorrows, which benefit no one, fret yourself, and dishonor your God? Why overburden yourself with forebodings?

"Hope in God," or "wait for God": there is need of patience, but there is ground for hope. The Heavenly Father will not stand by and see his children trampled upon forever; light must arise for the people of God, though for a while they may walk in darkness. Why, then, should we not be encouraged, and lift up our head with comfortable hope?

"For I shall yet praise him": times of complaint will soon end and seasons of praise begin.

"Who is the health of my countenance, and my God": my God will clear the furrows from my brow and the tear marks from my cheek; therefore will I smile in the face of the storm. The psalm has a blessed ending, such as we would like to imitate when death puts an end to our mortal existence.

CHAPTER TWO

A Plea for Renewal
Psalm 80

Verse 1. "Give ear, O Shepherd of Israel": the name is full of tenderness: broken hearts delight in names of grace. We may be quite sure that he who deigns to be a shepherd to his people will not turn a deaf ear to their complaints.

"Thou that leadest Joseph like a flock": the people are called here by the name of that renowned son who became a second father to the tribes, and kept them alive in Egypt; possibly they were known to the Egyptians under the name of "the family of Joseph."

"Thou that dwellest between the cherubims, shine forth": the Lord's special presence was revealed upon the mercy seat between the cherubim, and in all our pleadings we should come to the Lord by this way: only upon the mercy seat will God reveal his grace, and only there can we hope to commune with him. Let us ever plead the name of Jesus, who is our true mercy seat, to whom we may come boldly, and through whom we may look for a display of the glory of the Lord on our behalf. Our greatest dread is the withdrawal of the Lord's presence, and our brightest hope is the prospect of his return.

Verse 2. "Before Ephraim and Benjamin and Manasseh stir up thy strength, and come and save us." It is wise to mention the name of the Lord's people in prayer, for they are precious to him. Jesus bears the names of his people on his breastplate. Just as the mention of the names of his children has power with a father, so is it with the Lord. The prayer is that the God of Israel would be mighty on behalf of his people, chasing away their foes, and saving his people.

Verse 3. "Turn us again, O God": it is not so much said, "turn our captivity," but "turn us." All will come right if we are right. When the Lord turns his people he will soon turn their condition. It needs the Lord himself to do this, for conversion is as divine a work as creation; and those who have been once turned unto God, if they at any time backslide, as much need the Lord to turn them again as to turn them at the first. The word may be read, "restore us."

"And cause thy face to shine": be favorable to us; smile upon us. This was the high priest's blessing upon Israel: what the Lord has already given us by our High Priest and Mediator we may right confidently ask of him.

"And we shall be saved": all that is wanted for salvation is the Lord's favor. No matter how fierce the foe, or dire the captivity, the shining face of God ensures both victory and liberty. This verse is a very useful prayer, since we too often turn aside.

Verse 4. "O LORD God of hosts, how long wilt thou be angry against the prayer of thy people?" How long will the smoke of thy wrath drown the smoking incense of our prayers? Prayer would enter thy holy place, but thy wrath battles with it, and prevents its entrance. That God should be angry with us when sinning seems natural enough; that he should be angry even with our prayers is a bitter grief.

Verse 5. "Thou feedest them with the bread of tears": their meals, which were once such pleasant times of social merriment, are now like funeral feasts to which each person contributes a bitter morsel.

"And givest them tears to drink in great measure": not because their enemies have them in their power by force of arms, but because their God refuses to interpose; but it will by divine love be turned into a greater blessing by ministering to our spiritual health.

Verse 6. "Thou makest us a strife unto our neighbors": a neighbor's jeer is ever most cutting, especially if we have been superior to them, and claimed to possess more grace.

"And our enemies laugh among themselves": they find mirth in our misery, comedy in our tragedy, salt for their wit in the brine of our tears; it is the constant habit of the world to make merry with the saints' tribulations.

Verse 7. "Turn us again, O God of hosts." The prayer rises in the form of its address to God. He is here the God of Hosts. The more we approach the Lord in prayer and contemplation, the higher will our ideas of him become.

Verse 8. "Thou hast brought a vine out of Egypt": there it was in unfriendly soil: the waters of the Nile were as death to its shoots, while the inhabitants of the land despised it and trampled it down. Glorious was the right hand of the Lord when with power and great wonders he removed his pleasant place from the teeth of those who sought its destruction.

"Thou hast cast out the heathen, and planted it": seven nations were digged out to make space for the vine of the Lord; the old trees, which long had engrossed the soil, were torn up root and branch. The chosen vine was securely placed in its position with divine prudence and wisdom. Small in appearance, very dependent, exceeding weak, and apt to trail on the ground, yet the vine of Israel was chosen by the Lord, because he knew that by incessant care, and abounding skill, he could make of it a goodly fruitbearing plant.

Verse 9. "Thou preparedst room before it": the weeds, brambles, and huge stones were cleared; the Amorites, and their brothers in iniquity, were made to quit the scene, their forces were routed, their kings slain, their cities captured, and Canaan became like a plot of land made ready for a vineyard.

"And didst cause it to take deep root, and it filled the land": Israel became settled and established as a vine well rooted, and then it began to flourish and to spread on every side. This analogy might be applied to the experience of every believer in Jesus. The Lord has planted us, we are growing downward, "rooting roots," and by his grace we are also growing visibly bigger. The same is true of the church, for at this moment through the good will of the dresser of the vineyard her branches spread far and wide.

Verse 10. "The hills were covered with the shadow of it": Israel dwelt up to the mountain's summits, cultivating every foot of soil. The nation multiplied and became so great that other lands felt its influence, or were shadowed by it.

"And the boughs thereof were like the goodly cedars": the nation itself was so great that even its tribes were powerful and worthy to take rank among the mighty. A more correct rendering describes the cedars as covered with the vine, and we know that in many lands vines climb the trees, and cover them. In Solomon's time the little land of Israel occupied a high place among the nations. There have been times when the church of God also has been eminently conspicuous, and her power has been felt far and near.

Verse 11. "She sent out her boughs unto the sea": along the Mediterranean and, perhaps, across its waters, Israel's power was felt.

"And her branches unto the river": on her eastern side she pushed her commerce right to the Euphrates. Those were brave days for Israel, and would have continued, had not sin cut them short. When the church pleases the Lord, her influence becomes immense, far beyond the proportion which her numbers or her power would lead us to expect; but alas, when the Lord leaves her she becomes worthless.

Verse 12. "Why hast thou then broken down her hedges?" Thou hast withdrawn protection from her after caring for her with all this care; why is this, O Lord? A vine unprotected is exposed to every form of injury: such was Israel when given over to her enemies; such has the church often been.

"So that all they which pass by the way do pluck her." Her cruel neighbors have a pluck at her, and marauding bands, like roaming beasts, must pick at her. With God no enemy can harm us; without him none are so weak as to be unable to do us damage.

Verse 13. "The boar out of the wood doth waste it": such creatures are famous for rending and devouring vines. Fierce peoples, comparable to wild swine of the forest, warred with the Jewish nation, until it was gored and torn like a vine destroyed by greedy hogs.

"And the wild beast of the field doth devour it": first one foe and then another wreaked vengeance on the nation, and God did not interpose to chase them away. Ruin followed ruin. See what evils follow in the train of sin, and how terrible a thing it is for a people to be forsaken by God.

Verse 14. "Return, we beseech thee, O God of hosts." Turn thyself to us as well as us to thee. Thou hast gone from us because of our sins; come back to us, for we sigh and cry after thee. Or, if it be too much to ask thee to come, then do at least give us some consideration and cast an eye upon our griefs.

"Look down from heaven, and behold, and visit this vine." Do not close thine eyes; it is thy vine; at least note the mischief which the beasts have done, for then it may be thy heart will pity, and thy hand will be outstretched to deliver.

Verse 15. "And the vineyard which thy right hand hath planted": thou hast done so much; wilt thou lose thy labor? With thy power and wisdom thou didst great things for thy people, wilt thou now utterly give them up?

"And the branch that thou madest strong for thyself": a prayer for the leader whom the Lord had raised up, or for the Messiah whom they expected. Though the vine had been left, yet one branch had been regarded by the Lord, as if to furnish a scion for another vine. Let us pray the Lord, if he will not in the first place look upon his church, to look on the Lord Jesus, and then behold her in mercy for his sake.

Verse 16. "It is burned with fire": The vineyard was like a forest which has been set on fire; the choice vines were charred and dead.

"It is cut down": the cruel axe had hacked after its murderous fashion, the branches were lopped, the trunk was wounded, desolation reigned supreme.

"They perish at the rebuke of thy countenance": God's rebuke was to Israel what fire and axe would be to a vine. His wrath is as messengers of death.

Verse 17. "Let thy hand be upon the man of thy right hand": give a commission to some chosen man by whom thou wilt deliver. Honor him, save us, and glorify thyself. There is no doubt here an outlook to the Messiah, for whom believing Jews had learned to look as the Savior in time of trouble.

"Upon the son of man whom thou madest strong for thyself": send forth thy power with him whom thou shalt strengthen to accomplish thy purposes of grace. It is by the man Christ Jesus that fallen Israel is yet to rise, and indeed through him, who deigns to call himself the Son of Man, the world is to be delivered from the dominion of Satan and the curse of sin. O Lord, fulfill thy promise to the man of thy right hand, who participates in thy glory, and give him to see the pleasure of the Lord prospering in his hand.

Verse 18. "So will not we go back from thee." Under the leadership of one whom God had chosen the nation would be kept faithful, grace would work gratitude, and so cement them to their allegiance. It is in Christ that we abide faithful: because he lives we live also. There is no hope of our perseverance apart from him.

"Quicken us, and we will call upon thy name." If the Lord gives life out of death, his praise is sure to follow. The Lord Jesus is such a leader that in him is life, and the life is the light of men. When he visits our souls anew we shall be revivified, and our praise will ascend to the name of the Triune God.

Verse 19. "Turn us again, O LORD God of hosts": here we have another advance in the title, and the incommunicable name of Jehovah, the I AM, is introduced. Faith's prayers grow more full and mighty.

"Cause thy face to shine; and we shall be saved": even we who were so destroyed. No extremity is too great for the power of God. He is able to save at the last point, and that too by simply naming his smiling face upon his afflicted. People can do little, but God can do all things with a glance. Oh, to live forever in the light of his countenance!

CHAPTER THREE

God's Worshiping People, in Their Desperate Need, Pray
Psalm 85

Verse 1. "LORD, thou hast been favorable unto thy land." The self-existent, all-sufficient JEHOVAH is addressed: by that name he revealed himself to Moses when his people were in bondage. It is wise to dwell upon that view of the divine character which arouses the sweetest memories of his love. Sweeter still is that dear name of "Our Father," with which Christians have learned to commence their prayers. The psalmist speaks of Canaan as the Lord's land, for he chose it for his people, conveyed it by covenant to them, conquered it by his power, and dwelt in it in mercy. It is *our* land that is devastated, but O Jehovah, it is also *thy* land. The psalmist dwells upon the Lord's favor to the chosen land, which he had shown in a thousand ways. God's past doings are prophetic of what he will do; hence the encouraging argument: "thou hast been favorable to thy land," therefore deal graciously with it again.

"Thou hast brought back the captivity of Jacob." When oppressed through their sins, the ever-merciful One had chased away the invaders and given his people rest: this he had done not once, nor twice, but times without number. Many a time have we also been brought into soul-captivity by our backslidings, but we have not been left therein; the God who brought Jacob back from Padanaram to his father's house has restored us to the enjoyment of holy fellowship; will he not do the same again? Let us appeal to him with Jacob-like wrestlings, beseeching him to be favorable to us notwithstanding all our provocations. Let declining churches remember their former history, and with holy confidence plead with the Lord to turn their captivity yet again.

Verse 2. "Thou hast forgiven the iniquity of thy people." Often had he done this. Who is so slow to anger, so ready to forgive? Every believer in Jesus enjoys the blessing of pardoned sin, and should regard this as the pledge of all other needful mercies. He should plead it with God—"Lord, thou hast pardoned me, and wilt thou let me perish for lack of grace, or fall into thine enemies' hands? Thou wilt not thus leave thy work unfinished."

"Thou hast covered all their sin": all of it, every spot and wrinkle, the veil of love has covered. Covering it with the sea of the atonement, blotting it out, making it to cease to be, the Lord has put it away so completely that even his omniscient eye sees it no more. Not without a covering atonement is sin removed, but by means of the great sacrifice of our Lord Jesus, it is most effectually put away by one act, forever.

Verse 3. "Thou hast taken away all thy wrath." Having removed the sin, the anger is removed also. How often did the longsuffering of God take away from Israel the punishments which had been justly laid upon them! How often also has the Lord's chastising hand been removed from us when our waywardness called for heavier strokes!

"Thou hast turned thyself from the fierceness of thine anger." When ready to destroy, he had averted his face from his purpose of judgment and allowed mercy to interpose. The Book of Judges is full of illustrations of this, and the psalmist does well to quote them while he intercedes. Is not our experience equally studded with instances in which judgment has been stayed and tenderness has ruled? What a difference between the fierce anger which is feared and deprecated here, and the speaking of peace which is foretold in verse 8. There are many changes in Christians' experience, and therefore we must not despair when we are undergoing the drearier portion of the spiritual life, for soon, very soon, it may be transformed into gladness.

Verse 4. "Turn us, O God of our salvation": this was the main business. Could the erring tribes be rendered penitent, all would be well. It is not that God needs turning from his anger so much as that we need turning from our sin; here is the hinge of the whole matter. Our trials frequently arise out of our sins, but only God can turn us. When someone learns to pray for conversion there is hope for him: he who turns to prayer is beginning to turn from sin. It is a very blessed sight to see a whole people turn unto their God; may the Lord so send his converting grace on our land that we may live to see the people flocking to the loving worship of God.

"And cause thine anger toward us to cease": when sinners cease to rebel, the Lord ceases to be angry with them; when they return to him he returns to them; indeed, he is first in the reconciliation, and turns them when otherwise they would never turn of themselves.

Thus the psalmist asks for his nation priceless blessings, and quotes the best of arguments. Because the God of Israel has been so rich in favor in bygone years, he is entreated to reform and restore his backsliding nation.

Verse 5. "Wilt thou be angry with us for ever?" See how the psalmist makes bold to plead. We are in time as yet and not in eternity, and does not time come to an end, and therefore thy wrath? Wilt thou be angry always as if it were eternity? And if forever, yet wilt thou be angry "with us," thy favored people, the seed of Abraham, thy friend? That our enemies should be always angry is natural, but wilt *thou*, our God, be always incensed against us? Every word is an argument. Men in distress never waste words.

"Wilt thou draw out thine anger to all generations?" Will sons suffer for their fathers' faults, and punishment become an entailed inheritance? When we are under spiritual desertion we may beg in the same manner that the days of tribulation may be shortened, lest our spirit should utterly fail beneath the trial.

Verse 6. "Wilt thou not revive us again?" Hope here grows almost confident. We are dead or dying, faint and feeble; God alone can revive us; he has in other times refreshed his people; he is still the same; he will repeat his love. We appeal to him: "Wilt thou not?"

"That thy people may rejoice in thee." Thou lovest to see thy children happy with that best of happiness which centers in thyself; therefore revive us, for revival will bring us the utmost joy. Gratitude has an eye to the giver, even beyond the gift—

"thy people may rejoice *in thee*." Those who were revived would rejoice not only in the new life but in the Lord who was the author of it. Joy in the Lord is the ripest fruit of grace; all revivals and renewals lead up to it. By our possession of it we may estimate our spiritual condition. A genuine revival without joy is as impossible as spring without flowers, or daydawn without light.

Verse 7. "Show us thy mercy, O Lord." We cannot see it or believe it by reason of our long woes, but thou canst make it plain to us.

"And grant us thy salvation": this includes deliverance from the sin as well as the chastisement; it reaches from the depth of their misery to the height of divine love.

Verses 8-13. Having offered earnest intercession for the afflicted but penitent nation, the sacred poet in the true spirit of faith awaits a response from the sacred oracle. He pauses in joyful confidence, and then in ecstatic triumph he gives utterance to his hopes in the richest form of song.

Verse 8. "I will hear what God the Lord will speak." When we believe that God hears us, it is but natural that we should be eager to hear him. Only from him can come the word which can speak peace to troubled spirits. Happy is the supplicant who has grace to lie patiently at the Lord's door, and wait until his love acts according to its old custom and chase, all sorrow far away.

"For he will speak peace unto his people, and to his saints." Even though for a while his voice is stern with merited rebuke, the Father will reassume his natural tone of gentleness and pity. The speaking of peace is the peculiar prerogative of the

Lord Jehovah. Yet not to all does the divine word bring peace, but only to his own people, whom he means to make saints, and those whom he has already made so.

"But let them not turn again to folly": for if they do so, his rod will fall upon them again, and their peace will be invaded. Those who would enjoy communion with God must avoid all that would grieve the Holy Spirit; not only the grosser sins, but even the follies of life must be guarded against by those who are favored with the delights of conscious fellowship. Backsliders should study this verse with the utmost care; it will console them and yet warn them, draw them back to their allegiance and at the same time inspire them with a wholesome fear of going further astray. To turn again to folly is worse than being foolish once; it argues willfulness and obstinacy.

Verse 9. "Surely his salvation is nigh them that fear him": faith knows that a saving God is always near at hand, but *only* (for such is the true rendering) to those who fear the Lord, and worship him with holy awe. In the gospel dispensation this truth is conspicuously illustrated. If to seeking sinners salvation is nigh, it is assuredly very nigh to those who have once enjoyed it, and have lost its present enjoyment by their folly; they have but to turn unto the Lord and they will enjoy it again. We have not to go about by a long round of personal mortifications or spiritual preparations; we may come to the Lord Jesus Christ, just as we did at the first, and he will again receive us.

"That glory may dwell in our land": the object of the return of grace will be a permanent establishment of a better state of things, so that gloriously devout worship will be rendered to God continuously, and a glorious measure of prosperity will be enjoyed in consequence.

In these two verses we have, beneath the veil of the letter, an intimation of the coming of the Word of God to the nations in times of deep apostasy and trouble, when faithful hearts would be looking and longing for the promise which had so long tarried. By his coming, salvation is brought near.

Verse 10. "Mercy and truth are met together": the people recognize at once the grace and the veracity of Jehovah; he is to them neither a tyrant nor a deceiver.

"Righteousness and peace have kissed each other": the Lord, whose just severity inflicted the smart, now in pity sends peace to bind up the wound. The people being now made willing to forsake their sins, and to follow after righteousness, find peace granted to them at once.

This appears to be the immediate and primary meaning of these verses; but the inner sense is Christ Jesus, the reconciling Word. In him, the attributes of God unite in the salvation of guilty people. God is as true as if he had fulfilled every letter of his threatenings, as righteous as if he had never spoken peace to a sinner's conscience. It is the custom of modern thinkers to make sport of this representation of the result of our Lord's substitutionary atonement, but had they ever been themselves made to feel the weight of a sin upon a spiritually awakened conscience, they would cease from their vain ridicule.

Verse 11. "Truth shall spring out of the earth": promises which lie unfulfilled, like buried seeds, will spring up and yield harvests of joy; and people renewed by grace will learn to be true to one another and their God, and abhor the falsehood which they loved before.

"And righteousness shall look down from heaven": as if it threw up the windows and leaned out to gaze upon a penitent people, whom it could not have looked upon before without an indignation which would have been fatal to them.

In the person of our adorable Jesus Christ truth is found in our humanity, and his deity brings divine righteousness among us. There is a world of meaning in these verses, only needing meditation to draw it out. The well is deep, but if you have the Spirit, it cannot be said that you have nothing to draw with.

Verse 12. "Yea, the LORD shall give that which is good": being himself pure goodness, he will readily return from his wrath, and deal out good things to his repenting people. Our evil brings evil upon us, but when we are brought back to follow that which is good, the Lord abundantly enriches us with good things.

"And our land shall yield her increase": when the people yielded what was due to God, the soil would recompense their husbandry.

Verse 13. "Righteousness shall go before him; and shall set us in the way of his steps." God's march of right will leave a track his people will joyfully follow. He who smote in justice will also bless in justice, so as to affect the hearts and lives of all his people. Such are the blessings of our Lord's first advent, and such will be yet more conspicuously the result of his second coming.

PART 2

The Treasury of
the New Testament

CHAPTER FOUR

Our Need for Personal Revival

Through the power of the Holy Ghost
ROMANS 15:13

By the power of the Spirit of God
ROMANS 15:19

I desire to draw your attention at this time to the great necessity which exists for the continual manifestation of the power of the Holy Spirit in the church of God if by her means, the multitudes are to be gathered to the Lord Jesus. I felt I could much better do so by first showing that the Spirit of God is necessary to the church of God for its own internal growth in grace. Hence my text from Romans 15:13, "Now the God of hope fill you with all joy and peace in believing, that ye may abound in hope, through the power of the Holy Ghost." Here it is clear that the apostle attributes the power to be filled with joy and peace in believing, and the power to abound in hope, to the Holy Ghost. But, then, I wanted also to show you that the power of the church outside (that with which she is to be aggressive and work upon the world for the gathering out of God's elect from among men) is also this same energy of the Holy Spirit. Hence I have taken Romans 15:19 as well, where the apostle says that God had made through him "the Gentiles obedient by word and deed, through mighty signs and wonders, by the power of the Spirit of God."

So you see that first of all to keep the church happy and holy within herself there must be a manifestation of the power of the Holy Spirit. Secondly, so that the church may invade the territories of the enemy and may conquer the world for Christ, she must be clothed with the same sacred energy. We may then go further and say that the power of the church for external work will be proportionate to the power which dwells within herself. Gauge the energy of the Holy Spirit in the hearts of believers and you may fairly calculate their influence upon unbelievers. If the church is illuminated by the Holy Spirit, she will reflect the light and become to onlookers "fair as the moon, clear as the sun, and terrible as an army with banners" (Song of Solomon 6:4).

Let us look at a few illustrations that show the exterior work is always dependent on interior work. On a cold winter's day when the snow has fallen and lies deep on the ground, you go through a village. There is a row of cottages, and you notice that from one of the roofs the snow has nearly disappeared, while another cottage still bears a coating of snow. You do not stay to make inquiries as to the reason for the difference, for you know very well what is the cause. There is a fire burning inside the one cottage and the warmth glows through its roof, and so the snow speedily melts. In the other there is no tenant; it is a house for rent, no fire burns on its hearth, and no warm smoke ascends the chimney. Therefore there is snow on the roof. Just as there is warmth within so there will be melting outside. I look at a number of churches and I see worldliness and formalism lying thick on them. I am absolutely certain that there is no warmth of Christian life within; but where the hearts of believers are warm with divine love through the Spirit of God, we are sure to see evil vanish, and beneficial consequences coming from them. We need not look within; in such a case the exterior is a sufficient index.

Take an illustration from political life. Here trouble breaks out between different nations; there angry spirits arise. It seems very likely that the Gordian knot of difficulty will never be untied by diplomacy, but will need to be cut by the sword. Everybody knows that one of the hopes for peace lies in the bankrupt condition of the nation which is likely to go to war; for if it is short of supplies, if it cannot pay its debts, if it cannot furnish the material for war, then it will not be likely to court a conflict. A country must be strong in internal resources before it can wisely venture on foreign wars. Thus it is in the great battle for truth: a poor, starving church cannot fight the devil and its armies. Unless the church is herself rich in the things of God and strong with divine energy, she will cease to be aggressive, and will content herself with going on with the regular routine of Christian work, crying, "Peace, peace," where peace cannot exist. She will not dare to defy the world or to send out her legions to conquer its provinces for Christ, when her own condition is pitiably weak. The strength or weakness of a nation's treasure affects its army in every march, and in like manner its measure of grace influences the church of God in all its actions.

Here is a third illustration. If you lived in Egypt, you would notice that once a year the Nile rises. You would watch it rise with anxiety, because the extent of the overflow of the Nile is very much the measure of the fertility of Egypt. Now the rising of the Nile must depend on those distant lakes in central

Africa—whether they shall be well filled with the melting of the snows or not. If there is a small supply of water in the higher reservoirs, there cannot be much overflow in the Nile as it flows through Egypt. Let us translate this illustration. If the upper lakes of fellowship with God in the Christian church are not well filled—the Nile of practical Christian service will never rise to flood level.

The one thing I want to say is this: you cannot get of the church what is not in it. The reservoir itself must be filled before it can pour out a stream. We must ourselves drink from the living water until we are full, and then from us will flow rivers of living water; but not until then. You cannot distribute loaves and fishes out of an empty basket however hungry the crowd may be. Out of an empty heart you cannot speak about things that will feed God's people. Out of the fullness of the heart the mouth speaks, whenever it speaks to edify. So the first thing is to look well to home affairs and pray that God would bless us and have his face shine on us. Then, his way may be known on earth, and his saving health among all people.

> To bless Thy chosen race,
> In mercy, Lord, incline,
> And cause the brightness of Thy face
> On all Thy saints to shine.
> That so Thy wondrous way
> May through the world be known;
> While distant lands their tribute pay,
> And Thy salvation own.

In trying to speak about the great necessity of the church, being moved vigorously by the power of the Holy Spirit, I earnestly pray that we may enter into this subject with the deepest conceivable reverence. Let us adore God while we are meditating; let us feel the condescension of this blessed Person of the Godhead in deigning to live with his people and to work in the human heart. Let us remember that this divine person is very sensitive. He is a jealous God. We read of his being grieved and vexed, and, therefore, let us ask his forgiveness of the many provocations which he must have received from our hands. With lowliest awe let us bow before him, remembering that, if there is a sin which is unpardonable, it is the sin against the Holy Spirit, which will never be forgiven, neither in this world, nor in the next. In relation to the Holy Spirit we stand on very delicate ground indeed; and if we ever veil our faces and rejoice with trembling, it is while we speak of the Spirit, and of those mysterious works with which he blesses us. In that lowly spirit, and under the divine overshadowing, let me set before you seven works of the Holy Spirit which are most necessary to the church for its own good, and are equally needful to her in her office of missionary from Christ to the outside world.

1. The Holy Spirit quickens souls and brings spiritual life.
To begin, then, the power of the Holy Spirit is manifested in the quickening of souls, bringing them to spiritual life. All the spiritual life which exists in this world is the creation of the Holy Spirit and by him the Lord Jesus brings to spiritual life whoever he will. You and I did not have enough life to know that we were dead until he visited us. We did not have enough light to know that we were in darkness, nor sense enough to feel our misery. We were so utterly abandoned to our own folly that though we were naked, and poor, and miserable, we thought that we were rich and increased in goods. We were

under sentence of death as condemned criminals, and yet we talked about merit and reward. Yes, we were dead, and yet we boasted that we were alive, counting our very death as if it were life. This Spirit of God in infinite mercy came to us with his mysterious power and made us live. The first indication of life was a consciousness of our being in the realm of death, and a desire to escape from it. We began to perceive our insensibility, and, if I may be pardoned such an expression, we saw our blindness. Every growth of spiritual life, from the first tender shoot until now, has also been the work of the Holy Spirit. As the green blade was produced by him, so is the ripening corn. The increase of life, as much as life at the beginning, must still come through the work of the Spirit of God, who raised up Christ from the dead. You will only have more life, Christian friend, as the Holy Spirit bestows it on you. In fact, you will not even know that you want more, or seek more, unless he works in you to initiate this desire. Note, then, our absolute dependence on the Holy Spirit; for if he were going we should relapse into spiritual death, and the church would become a cemetery.

The Holy Spirit is absolutely necessary to make everything that we do come to life. We are sowers, but if we use dead seed in our seed-basket there will never be a harvest. The preacher must preach living truth in a living manner if he expects to receive a hundred-fold harvest. There is much of church work which is nothing better than the movement of a galvanized corpse. Much religion is done as if it were performed like a piece of automatic machinery. Nowadays people care little about the heart and soul, they only look at exterior performance. We can preach as machines, we can pray as machines, and we can teach Sunday school as machines. People can give mechanically and come to the communion table mechanically and we will do so unless the Spirit of God is with us. Most listeners know what it is to hear a live sermon which quivers all over with energy; they also know what it is to sing a hymn in a lively manner, and they know what it is to unite in a live prayer meeting; but if the Spirit of God is absent, all that the church does will be lifeless, a rustling of leaves above a tomb, the congregation of the dead turning over in their graves.

As the Spirit of God is a quickener to make us alive and our work alive, so must he especially be with us to make alive those with whom we speak of Jesus. Imagine a dead preacher preaching a dead sermon to dead sinners: what can possibly come of that? In that case there is a beautiful essay which has been admirably elaborated, and is coldly read to the cold hearted sinner. It smells of the midnight oil, but it has no heavenly unction, no divine power resting on it, nor, perhaps, is that power even looked for. What good can come from such a production? We may as well try to calm the storm with poetry or stay the hurricane with rhetoric as to bless a soul by mere learning and eloquence. It is only as the Spirit of God shall come on God's servant and make the word which he preaches to drop as a living seed into the heart that any result can follow his ministry; and it is only as the Spirit of God will then follow that seed and keep it alive in the soul of the listener that we can expect those who profess to be converted to take root and grow to maturity of grace, and become our sheaves at the last.

We are utterly dependent here, and for my part, I rejoice in this absolute dependence. If I could have a stock of power to save souls which would be all my own apart from the Spirit of God, I cannot suppose a greater temptation to pride and to living at a distance from God. It is well to be weak in self, and better still to be nothing: to be simply the pen in the hand of the Spirit of God, unable to write a single letter on the tablets of the human heart except as the hand of the Holy Spirit will use us for that purpose. That is really our position, and we ought practically to take it up; and doing so we shall continually cry to the Spirit of God to quicken us in all things, and quicken all that we do, and quicken the word as it drops into the sinner's ear. I am quite certain that a church which is devoid of life cannot be the means of life-giving to the dead sinners around it. No. Everything acts after its own kind, and we must have a living church for living work. O that God would quicken every member of this church! "What," you reply, "do you think some of us are not alive to God?" Christian friends, there are some of you about whom I am certain, as far as one can judge another person, that you have life, for we can see it in all that you do; but there are some others of you about whose spiritual life one has to exercise a good deal of faith and a great deal more charity, for we do not perceive in you much activity in God's cause, nor concern about other people's souls, nor zeal for the divine glory. If we do not see any fruits, what can we do but earnestly pray that you may not turn out to be barren trees?

That is the first point, and we think it is as clear as possible that we must have the quickening power of the Spirit for ourselves if we are to be the means in the hand of God of awakening dead souls.

2. The Holy Spirit enlightens his people.

Next, it is one of the special offices of the Holy Spirit to enlighten his people. He has done so by giving us his word, which he has inspired; but the Book, inspired though it is, is never spiritually understood by anyone apart from the personal teaching of its great Author. You may read it as much as you will, and never discover the inner and vital sense unless your soul will be led into it by the Holy Spirit himself. "What," someone replies, "I have learned the Shorter Catechism and I know the creed by heart, and yet do I know nothing?" I answer, you have done well to learn the letter of truth, but you still need the Spirit of God to make it the light and power of God to your soul. The letter you may know, and know it better than some who know also the spirit, and I do not for a moment depreciate a knowledge of the letter, unless you suppose that there is something saving in mere head knowledge; but the Spirit of God must come, and make the letter alive to you, transfer it to your heart, set it on fire and make it burn within you, or else its divine force and majesty will be hidden from your eyes. No one knows the things of God except the person to whom the Spirit of God has revealed them. No earthly mind can understand spiritual things. We may use language as plain as a pikestaff, but the man who has no spiritual understanding is a blind man, and the clearest light will not enable him to see. You must be taught by the Lord, or you will die in ignorance. Now, suppose that in a church there should be many who have never been instructed in this way. Can you not see that evil must and will come from it? Error is sure to arise where truth is not experimentally known. If professors are not taught from the Spirit, their ignorance will breed conceit, pride, unbelief, and a thousand other evils. Oh, had you known more about truth, my Christian friend, you would not have boasted in this way! If you had seen the truth, which up to now has not been revealed to you because of your prejudice, you would not have so fiercely condemned those who are better than yourself.

With much zeal to do good, people have done a world of harm through lack of instruction in divine things. Sorrow, too, comes from ignorance. O, my brother, if only you had known the doctrines of grace you would have not been so long in bondage. Half of the heresy in God's church is not willful error, but error which springs from not knowing the truth, not searching the Scriptures with a teachable heart, not submitting the mind to the light of the Holy Spirit. We should, as a rule, treat heresy rather as ignorance to be enlightened than as crime to be condemned; unless, alas, that sometimes it becomes willful perversity, when the mind is greedy after novelty, or puffed up with self-confidence; then another treatment may become painfully necessary. Beloved, if the Spirit of God will but enlighten the church thoroughly there will be an end of division. Schisms are generally brought about by ignorance, and the proud spirit which will brook no correction. On the other hand, real, lasting, practical unity will exist in proportion to the unity of men's minds in the truth of God. Hence it is necessary for the Spirit of God to conduct us into the whole truth. My dear brother, if you think you know a doctrine, ask the Lord to make you sure that you know it, for much that we think we know turns out to be unknown when times of trial put us to the test. Nothing do we really know unless it is burnt into our souls as with a hot iron by an experience which only the Spirit of God can give.

I think you will see that the Spirit of God is necessary for our instruction. Then we find in this gracious work our strength for the instruction of others. For how can people teach who have not been taught? How can people declare a message they have not learned? "Son of man, eat this roll"; for until you have eaten it yourself your lips can never tell it to others. "The husbandman that laboreth must first be a partaker of the fruits." It is the law of Christ's vineyard that no one will work there until they know the flavor of the fruits which grow in the sacred enclosure. You must know Christ, and grace, and love, and truth yourself before you can even be a teacher of babes for Christ.

When we come to deal with others, earnestly longing to instruct them for Jesus, we perceive even more clearly our need of the Spirit of God. Ah, my brother, you think you will put the gospel so clearly that they must see it; but their blind eyes overcome you. Ah, you think you will put it so zealously that they must feel it; but their clay-cold hearts defeat you. You may think that you are going to win souls by your pleadings, but you might as well stand on top of a mountain and whistle to the wind, unless the Holy Spirit is with you. After all your talking your hearers will, perhaps, have caught your idea, but the mind of the Spirit, the real soul of the gospel, you cannot impart to them; this remains like creation itself, a work which only God can accomplish. Daily, then, let us pray for the power of the Spirit as the Illuminator. Come, O blessed light of God. You alone can break our personal darkness, and only when you have enlightened us can we lead others in your light. An ignorant Christian is disqualified for great usefulness; but he who is taught from God will teach transgressors God's ways, and sinners will be converted to Christ. Both to burn within and shine without you must have the illuminating Spirit.

3. The Holy Spirit is the spirit of adoption.

One work of the Holy Spirit is to create in believers the spirit of adoption. "Because ye are sons, God hath sent forth the Spirit of his Son into your hearts, whereby ye cry, Abba, Father!" "For ye have not received the spirit of bondage again to fear, but ye have received the spirit of adoption, whereby we cry, Abba, Father!" We are regenerated by the Holy Spirit, and so receive the nature of children; and that nature, which is given by him, he continually prompts, and excites, and develops, and matures; so that we receive day by day more and more of the childlike spirit. Now, beloved, this may not seem to you to be of great importance at first sight, but it is so for the church is never happy except as all her members walk as dear children towards God. Sometimes the spirit of slaves creeps over us: we begin to talk of God's service as if it were heavy and burdensome, and are discontented if we do not receive visible success. But the spirit of adoption works for love, without any hope of reward, and it is satisfied with the sweet fact of being in the Father's house, and doing the Father's will. This spirit gives peace, rest, joy, boldness, and holy familiarity with God. A man who never received the spirit of a child towards God does not know the blessing of the Christian life; he misses its flower, its savor, its excellence, and I should not wonder if the service of Christ should be weariness to him because he has never yet come to the sweet things, and does not enjoy the green pastures, wherein the Good Shepherd makes his sheep feed and lie down. But when the Spirit of God makes us feel that we are sons and daughters, and we live in the house of God to go no more out forever, then God's service is sweet and easy, and we accept the delay of apparent success as a part of the trial we are called to bear.

Now, mark you, this will have a great effect on the outside world. A body of professors performing religion as a task, groaning along the ways of godliness with faces full of misery, like slaves who dread the lash, can have but small effect upon the sinners around them. They say, "These people serve, no doubt, a hard master, and they are denying themselves this and that. Why should we be like them?" But bring me a church made up of God's children, a company of men and women whose faces shine with their heavenly Father's smile, who are accustomed to take their cares and cast them on their Father as children should, who know they are accepted and beloved, and are perfectly content with the great Father's will; put them down in the middle of a group of ungodly people, and I will guarantee that they will begin to be jealous of their peace and joy. In this way happy saints become the most effective workers on the minds of the unsaved. O blessed Spirit of God! Let us all now feel that we are the children of the great Father, and let our childlike love be warm today; so shall we be fit to go and proclaim the Lord's love to the prodigals who are in the distant land among the pigs.

These three points are self-evident, I think. Now I move on to the fourth point.

4. The Holy Spirit is the Spirit of holiness.
The Holy Spirit is especially called the Spirit of holiness. He never suggested sin nor approved of it, nor has he ever done other than grieve over it. But holiness is the Spirit's delight. God's church wears upon her brow the words, "Holiness to the Lord." Only in proportion as she is holy may she claim to be the church of God at all. An unholy church! Surely this cannot be her about whom we read, "Christ also loved the church, and gave himself for it; that he might sanctify and cleanse it with the washing of water by the word, that he might present it to himself a glorious church, not having spot, or wrinkle, or any such thing."

Holiness is not mere morality, not the outward keeping of divine precepts out of a strong sense of duty, while those commandments in themselves are not our delight. Holiness is our complete being fully consecrated to the Lord and molded to his will. This is the thing which God's church must have, but it can never have it apart from the Sanctifier, for there is not a grain of holiness beneath the sky but what is of the work of the Holy Spirit. And, brethren, if a church is destitute of holiness what effect can it have on the world? Scoffers utterly condemn and despise people who live inconsistent lives which contradict their verbal testimonies. An unholy church may pant and struggle after dominion, and make what noise she can in pretense of work for Christ, but the kingdom comes not to the unholy, neither have they themselves entered it! The testimony of unholy men is no more acceptable to Christ than was the homage which the evil spirit gave to him in the days of his flesh, to which he answered, "Hold thy peace." "Unto the wicked God saith, What hast thou to do to declare my statutes?" The dew is withholden, and the rain cometh not in its season to those who profess to be God's servants and yet sow iniquity. After all, the deeds of the church preach more to the world than the words of the church. Put an anointed man to preach the gospel in the middle of really godly people and his testimony will be wonderfully supported by the church with which he labors; but place the most faithful minister over an ungodly church, and he has such a weight on him that he must first rid himself of it, or he cannot succeed. He may preach his heart out, he may pray till his knees are weary, but conversions will be sorely hindered, if indeed they occur at all. There is no likelihood of victory to Israel while Achan's curse is on the camp. An unholy church makes Christ say that he cannot do many mighty works there because of its iniquity.

Brethren, do you not see in this point our need of the Spirit of God? And when you get to grappling with sinners, and talk to them about the necessity of holiness, and a renewed heart, and a godly life coming out of that renewed heart, do you expect ungodly men to be charmed with what you say? What cares the unregenerate mind for righteousness? Was an earthly person ever eager for holiness? Such a thing was never seen. We might as well expect the devil to be in love with God as an unredeemed heart to be in love with holiness. But yet the sinner must love that which is pure and right, or he cannot enter heaven. You cannot make him do so. Who can do it but that Holy Spirit who has made you to love what once you also despised? Do not go out, therefore, to battle with sin until you have taken weapons out of the armory of the eternal Spirit. Mountains of sin will not turn to plains at your bidding unless the Holy Spirit is pleased to make the word effectual. So then we see that for the Spirit of holiness we need the Holy Spirit.

5. The Holy Spirit is the Spirit of supplication.

The church needs much prayer, and the Holy Spirit is the Spirit of grace and of supplication. The strength of a church may be accurately gauged by her prayerfulness. We cannot expect God to put forth his power unless we entreat him to do so. But all acceptable supplication is wrought in the soul by the Holy Spirit. The first desire which God accepts must have been excited in the heart by the secret work of the Holy One of Israel; and every subsequent pleading of every sort which contains in it a grain of living faith, and therefore comes up as a memorial before the Lord, must have been effectually wrought in the soul by him who makes intercession in the saints according to the will of God. Our great High Priest will put into his censer no incense but that which the Spirit has compounded. Prayer is the creation of the Holy Spirit. We cannot do without prayer, and we cannot pray without the Holy Spirit; and hence our dependence on him.

Furthermore, when we come to deal with sinners, we know that they must pray. "Behold he prayeth" is one of the earliest signs of the new birth. But can we make the sinner pray? Can any persuasion of ours lead him to his knees to breathe the penitential sigh and look to Christ for mercy? If you have attempted the conversion of a soul in your own strength you know you have failed; and so you would have failed if you had attempted the creation of one single acceptable prayer in the heart of even a little child. Oh, then, dear brethren, let us cry to our heavenly Father to give the Holy Spirit to us; let us ask him to be in us more and more mightily as the spirit of prayer, making intercession in us with groanings that cannot be uttered, that the church may not miss the divine blessing for lack of asking for it. I do truly believe that this is the present weakness, and one great reason why the kingdom of Christ does not more mightily spread; prayer is too much restrained, and hence the blessing is held back; and it will always be restrained unless the Holy Spirit stimulates the desires of his people.

O blessed Spirit, we pray thee make us pray, for Jesus' sake.

6. The Holy Spirit is the giver of fellowship.

The Spirit of God is in a very remarkable way the giver of fellowship. So often as we pronounce the apostolic benediction we pray that we may receive the communion of the Holy Spirit. The Holy Spirit enables us to have communion with spiritual things. He alone can take the key and open up the secret mystery, that we may know the things which are of God. He gives us fellowship with God himself; through Jesus Christ by the Spirit we have access to the Father. Our fellowship is with the Father, and with his Son Jesus Christ, but it is the Spirit of God who brings us into communion with the Most High.

So, too, my dear brethren, our fellowship with one another, so far as it is Christian fellowship, is always produced by the Spirit of God. If we have continued together in peace and love these many years, I cannot attribute it to our constitutional good tempers, nor to wise management, nor to any natural causes, but to the love into which the Spirit has baptized us, so that rebellious nature has been still. If a dozen Christian people live together for twelve months in true spiritual union and unbroken affection, trace it to the love of the Spirit; and if a dozen hundred, or four times that number, will be able to persevere in united service, and find themselves loving each other better after many years than they did at the beginning, let it be seen as a blessing from the Comforter, for which he is to be devoutly adored. Fellowship can only come to us by the Spirit, but a church without fellowship would be a disorderly mob, a kingdom divided against itself, and consequently it could not prosper. You need fellowship for mutual strength, guidance, help, and encouragement, and without it your church is a mere human society.

If you are to tell the Christian message to the world you must be united as one living body. Divisions are our disgrace, our weakness, our hindrance, and as the gentle Spirit alone can prevent or heal these divisions by giving us real loving fellowship with God and with one another, how dependent we are upon him for it. Let us daily cry to him to work in us brotherly love, and all the sweet graces which make us one with Christ, that we all may be one even as the Father is one with the Son, that the world may know that God hath indeed sent Jesus, and that we are his people.

7. The Holy Spirit is the Paraclete, or Comforter.

We need the Holy Spirit in that renowned office which is described by our Lord as the Paraclete, or Comforter. The word bears another translation, "If any man sin we have an Advocate (or Paraclete) with the Father." The Holy Spirit is both Comforter and Advocate.

The Holy Spirit at this present moment is our Friend and Comforter, sustaining the sinking spirits of believers, applying the precious promises, revealing the love of Jesus Christ to the heart. Many a heart would break if the Spirit of God had not comforted it. Many of God's dear children would have utterly died by the way if he had not bestowed on them his divine consolations to cheer their pilgrimage. That is his work, and a very necessary work, for if believers become unhappy, they become weak in God's service. I am certain that the joy of the Lord is our strength, for I have proved it so, and proved also the opposite truth. There are on earth certain Christians who inculcate gloom as a Christian's proper state. I will not judge them, but this I will say, that in evangelistic work they do nothing, and I do not wonder. Till snow in harvest ripens wheat, till darkness makes flowers blossom, till the salt sea yields clusters bursting with new wine, you will never find an unhappy religion promotive of the growth of the kingdom of Christ. You must have joy in the Lord, brethren, if you are strong in the Lord, and strong for the Lord. Now, as the Comforter alone can bear you up in the middle of floods of tribulation which you are sure to meet with, you see your great need of his consoling presence.

We have said that the Spirit of God is the Advocate of the church—not with God, for there Christ is our sole Advocate, but with man. What is the grandest plea that the church has against the world? I answer, the indwelling of the Holy Spirit, the standing miracle of the church. External evidences are very excellent. You young men who are troubled by skeptics will do well to study those valuable works which learned and devout men have with much labor produced for us; but note, all the evidences of the truth of Christianity which can be gathered from analogy, from history, and from external facts are nothing when compared with the work of the Spirit of God. These are the arguments which convince.

A man says to me, "I do not believe in sin, in righteousness, or in judgment." Well, brethren, the Holy Spirit can soon convince him. If he asks me for signs and evidences of the truth of the gospel, I reply, "Seest thou this woman? She was a great sinner in the very worst sense, and led others into sin, but now you cannot find more sweetness and light anywhere than in her. Listen to this profane swearer and persecutor. Now he is speaking with purity, truth, and humility. Note that man who used to be a miser but who now is glad to give generously. Notice that envious, malicious spirit, and see how it becomes gentle, forgiving, and amiable through conversion. How do you account for these great changes? They are happening here every day; how do they take place? Is that a lie which produces truth, honesty, and love? Does not every tree bear fruit after its kind? What is the grace that produces such wonderful transformations? The amazing phenomena of ravens turned to doves, and lions into lambs, the marvelous transformations of moral character which the minister of Christ rejoices to see performed by the gospel, these are our witnesses, and they are unanswerable."

Peter and John have gone up to the temple, and they have healed a lame man; they are soon seized and brought before the Sanhedrin. This is the charge against them—"You have been preaching in the name of Jesus, and this Jesus is an impostor." What do Peter and John say? They need say nothing, for there stands the man who was healed; he has brought his crutch with him, and he waves it in triumph, and he runs and leaps. He was their volumes of evidence, their apology, and proof. "When they saw the man who was healed standing with Peter and John, they could say nothing against them."

If we have the Spirit of God among us, and conversions are constantly being performed, the Holy Spirit is thus fulfilling his advocacy and refuting all accusers. If the Spirit works in your own mind, it will always be to you the best evidence of the gospel. I meet sometimes one piece of infidelity, and then another; for there are new doubts and fresh infidelities spawned every hour, and unstable men expect us to read all the books they choose to produce. But the effect produced on our mind is less and less. This is our answer. It is no use you trying to stagger us, for we are already familiar with everything you suggest; our own native unbelief has outstripped you. We have had doubts of a kind which even you would not dare to utter if you knew them; for there is enough unfaithfulness and satanic activity in our own nature to make us no strangers to the devil's devices. We have fought most of your suggested battles over and over again in the secret chamber of meditation and have conquered. For we have been in personal contact with God. You sneer, but there is no argument in sneering. We are as honest as you are, and our witness is as good as yours in any court of law; and we solemnly declare that we have felt the power of the Holy Spirit over our soul as much as the old ocean has ever felt the force of the north wind. We have been stirred to agony under a sense of sin, and we have been lifted to ecstasy of delight by faith in the righteousness of Christ. We find that in the little world within our soul the Lord Jesus manifests himself so that we know him. There is a potency about the doctrines we have learned which could not belong to lies, for the truths which we believe we have tested in actual experience. Tell us there is no meat? Why, we have just been feasting. Tell us there is no water in the fountain? We have been quenching our thirst. Tell us there is no such thing as light? We do not know how we can prove its existence to you, for you are probably blind, but we can see. That is enough argument for us, and our witness is true. Tell us there is no spiritual life? We feel it in our inmost souls. There are the answers with which the Spirit of God furnishes us, and they are part of his advocacy.

See, again, how entirely dependent we are on the Spirit of God for meeting all the various forms of unbelief which arise around us; you may have your societies for collecting evidence, and you may enlist all your bishops and doctors of divinity and professors of apologetics, and they may write rolls of evidence long enough to wrap round the earth, but the only person who can savingly convince the world is the Advocate whom the Father has sent in the name of Jesus. When he reveals a person's sin, and the sure result of it, the unbeliever takes to his knees. When he takes away the scales and sets forth the crucified Redeemer, and the merit of the precious blood, all earthly reasonings are nailed to the cross. One blow of real conviction of sin will stagger the most obstinate unbeliever, and afterwards, if his unbelief returns, the Holy Spirit's consolations will soon comfort it out of him. Therefore, as I said to start with, so I conclude by saying, all this depends on the Holy Spirit, and upon him let us wait in the name of Jesus, beseeching him to show his power among us. Amen.

CHAPTER FIVE

Pleasing the Holy Spirit in Revival

And grieve not the Holy Spirit of God,
whereby ye are sealed unto the day of redemption
EPHESIANS 4:30

There is something very touching in this admonition, "Grieve not the Holy Spirit of God." It does not say, "Do not make him angry." A more delicate and tender term is used—"Grieve him not." There are some people who have such hard characters that they feel no pain when they upset other people. Indeed, some of us are hardly moved when we know that we have been the cause of upsetting others. But where is the heart so hard that it is not moved when we know that we have caused others grief? For grief is a sweet combination of anger and love. It is anger, but all the gall is taken from it. Love sweetens the anger, and turns the edge of it, not against the person, but against the offense. We all know how we use the terms. When I commit any offense, some friend who has but little patience suddenly snaps and becomes angry with me. The same offense is observed by a loving father, and he is grieved. There is anger in his heart, but he is angry and he sins not for he is angry against my sin; and yet there is love to neutralize and modify the anger towards me. Instead of wishing me ill as the punishment of my sin, he looks upon my sin itself as being the cause. He grieves to think that I am already injured from the fact that I have sinned. I call this a heavenly medicine because it is more precious than all the ointments of merchants. There may be the bitterness of myrrh, but there is all the sweetness of frankincense in this sweet term "to grieve."

I am certain that I do not flatter you when I declare that I am sure that most of you would grieve if you thought that you were grieving someone else. You, perhaps, would not care much if you had made someone angry when there was no real need for anger, but to grieve him, even though it might be unintentionally, would nevertheless cause you distress of heart. You would not rest until the grief had subsided, until you had made some explanation or apology and had done your best to take away the cause of grief.

When we see anger in somebody else, we at once begin to feel hostility. Anger begets anger; but grief begets compassion, and compassion is like love; and we love those whom we have caused grief. Now, is this not a very sweet expression—"Grieve not the Holy Spirit"? The Holy Spirit of God's emotion is here described, in human language, as being that of grief. Is it not a tender and touching thing that the Holy Spirit should direct his servant Paul to say to us, "Grieve not the Holy Spirit," do not excite his loving anger, do not vex him, do not cause him to mourn? He is a dove; do not cause him to mourn, because you have treated him harshly and ungratefully.

As I exhort you not to grieve the Holy Spirit, I shall divide my sermon into three headings: first, the love of the Holy Spirit; second, the seal of the Holy Spirit; and, third, grieving the Holy Spirit.

1. The love of the Holy Spirit.

The few words I have to say about the love of the Holy Spirit will help to stir you up not to grieve the Holy Spirit. For when we are persuaded that another person loves us, we find at once a very potent reason why we should not grieve him. The love of the Spirit—how can I explain this? Surely it needs a singer to sing it, for love is only to be spoken about in words of song. The love of the Spirit—let me tell you about his early love for us. He loved us without beginning. In the eternal covenant of grace, he was one of the parties in the divine plan by which we are saved. All that can be said about the love of the Father, or the love of the Son, may be said about the love of the Spirit— it is eternal, it is infinite, it is sovereign, it is everlasting; it is a love that cannot be dissolved, which cannot be lessened, a love which cannot be removed from those who are its objects.

Permit me, however, to refer you to his acts, rather than to his attributes. Let me tell you about the love of the Spirit to you and to me. Oh, how early was that love which he showed towards us, even in our childhood. My brethren, we can well remember how the Spirit engaged us. We went astray from birth, telling lies, but how early did the Spirit of God stir up our conscience, and solemnly correct us on account of our youthful sins. How frequently since then has the Spirit wooed us! How often has he compelled our hearts to melt, the tear to run down our cheeks, and he has sweetly whispered in our ear, "My son, give me thy heart; go to thy chamber, shut thy door about thee, confess thy sins, and seek a Savior's love and blood."

Oh, but let us blush to tell it—how often have we turned against him. When we were in a state of being unregenerate, how often we resisted him. We quenched the Spirit. He engaged with us, but we fought against him. But blessed be his dear name, and let him have everlasting songs for it, he would not let us go. We did not want to be saved, but he desired to save us. We sought to thrust ourselves into the fire, but he sought to pluck us from the burning flames. We would throw ourselves over the precipice, but he fought to hold on to us. He would not let us destroy our souls. How we ill-treated him! We ignored his counsel. We scoffed at him; we scorned him and we despised the ordinances which would lead us to Christ. How we tugged at that holy cord which was gently drawing us to Jesus and his cross! I am certain that as you recall your rebellion against the Holy Spirit you must be stirred to love him.

How often did he restrain you from sin when you were about to plunge headlong into some evil action? How often did he persuade you to do good when you wanted to neglect a kind deed? You, perhaps, would not have been in the Christian way at all, and the Lord would not have met you, if it had not been for that sweet Spirit, who would not let you become a blasphemer, who would not allow you to forsake the house of God, and would not permit you to become a regular visitor to the haunts of vice, but checked you and held you in, as it were, with bit and bridle. Though you were like a bullock, unaccustomed to a yoke, he would not let you have your own way. Though you struggled against him, he said, "I will have him, I will have him against his will; I will change his heart, I will not let him go until I have made him a trophy of my mighty power to save." And then think of the love of the Spirit after that—

> Dost mind the time, the spot of land,
> Where Jesus did thee meet?
> Where he first took thee by the hand,
> Thy Bridegroom's love—how sweet!

Ah, then, in that happy moment, dear to the memory, was it not the Holy Spirit who guided you to Jesus? Do you remember the love of the Spirit, when, after you were brought alive, he took you aside and showed you Jesus on the tree? Who was it that opened your blind eye to see a dying Savior? Who was it that opened your deaf ear to hear the voice of pardoning love? Who opened your clasped and palsied hand to receive the tokens of a Savior's grace? Who was it that broke your hard heart and made a way for the Savior to enter and live there? Oh, it was the precious Spirit, that self-same Spirit, whom you had rejected, whom in previous days you had resisted! What a mercy it was that he did not say, "I will swear in my wrath that they shall not enter into my rest, for they have vexed me, and I will take my everlasting flight from them"; or thus, "Ephraim is joined unto idols, I will let him alone!"

Since that time, my brethren, how sweetly has the Spirit proved his love to you and to me. It is not only in his first strivings, and then his divine quickenings; but in all the sequel, how much have we owed to his instruction! We have been dull scholars with the word before us, plain and simple, so that he that runs may read, and he that reads may understand, yet how small a portion of his word has our memory retained—how little progress have we made in the school of God's grace! We are but learners yet, unstable, weak, and apt to slide, but what a blessed instructor we have had! Has he not led us into many a truth, and taken the things of Christ and applied them to us? Oh, when I think how stupid I have been, I wonder that he has not given up on me. When I think what a stupid person I have been, when he would have taught me about the kingdom of God, I marvel that he should have had such patience with me. Is it a wonder that Jesus should become a baby? Is it not an equal wonder that the Spirit of the living God should become a teacher of babies? It is a marvel that Jesus should lie in a manger; is it not an equal marvel that the Holy Spirit should become an usher in the sacred school, to teach fools, and make them wise? It was condescension that brought the Savior to the cross, but is it not equal condescension that brings the mighty Spirit of grace down to live with stubborn, unruly, wild asses' colts, to teach them the mystery of the kingdom, and make them know the wonders of a Savior's love?

Furthermore, my brethren, forget not how much we owe to the Spirit's consolation, how much he has shown his love to you in cherishing you in all your sicknesses, assisting you in all your labors; and comforting you in all your distresses. He has been a blessed comforter to me I can testify; when every other comfort failed, when the promise itself seemed empty, when the ministry was void of power, it is then the Holy Spirit has proved a rich comfort to my soul, and filled my poor heart with peace and joy in believing. How many times would your heart have broken if the Spirit had not bound it up! How often has he who is your teacher become also your physician, has closed the wounds of your poor bleeding spirit, and has bound up those wounds with his promises, and has returned your spiritual health to you!

It does seem to me a marvel that the Holy Spirit should become a comforter, for comforting is, to many minds, but an inferior work in the church, though really it is not so. To teach, to preach, to command with authority, how many are willing to do this because this is honorable work; but to sit down and bear with the infirmities of the creature, to enter into all the strategies of unbelief, to find the soul a way of peace in the middle of seas of trouble—this is compassion like

God, the comforter of disconsolate spirits. What? Must he himself bring the medicine? Must he wait on his sick child and stand by his bed? Must he make his bed for him in his affliction? Must he carry him in his sickness? Must he breathe continually into him his own breath? Does the Holy Spirit become a waiting servant of the church? Does he become a staff on which we may lean? This, I say, should move us to love the Holy Spirit, for we have in all this, abundant proofs of his love for us.

Do not stay here, beloved, there are larger fields yet beyond, now that we are speaking about the love of the Spirit. Remember how much he loves us when he helps our sicknesses. But also remember that he assists us in our praying, when we do not know what to pray for, when "we ourselves groan within ourselves," then the Spirit himself makes intercession for us with groanings which cannot be uttered— groans as we should groan, but more audibly, so that our prayer, which otherwise would have been silent, reaches the ears of Christ, and is then presented before his Father's face.

To help our infirmities is a mighty instance of love. When God overcomes infirmity altogether, or removes it, there is something very noble, and grand, and sublime in the deed; when he permits the infirmity to remain and yet works with the infirmity, this is tender compassion indeed. When the Savior heals the lame man, you see his Godhead; but when he walks with the lame man, limping though his walk is, then you see a manifestation of love almost unequaled. Except for Christ bearing our infirmities and sins on the tree, I know of no greater or more tender instance of divine love than when it is written: "Likewise the Spirit also helpeth our infirmities." Oh, how much you owe to the Spirit when you have been on your knees in prayer! You know, my brethren, what it is to be dull and lifeless there; to groan for a word, and yet the very wish is languid; to long to have desires, and yet all the desire you have is a desire that you may be able to desire. Oh, have you not sometimes, when your desires have kindled, longed to get a grip at the promise by the hand of faith? "Oh," you have said, "if I could but plead the promise, all my necessities would be removed, and all my sorrows would be allayed," but, alas, the promise was beyond your reach. If you touched it with the tip of your finger, you could not grasp it as you desired, you could not plead it, and therefore you came away without the blessing. But when the Spirit has helped our infirmities how have we prayed! Why, there have been times when you and I have so grasped the knocker of the gate of mercy, and have let it fall with such tremendous force, that it seemed as if the very gate itself did shake and totter; there have been seasons when we have laid hold on the angel, have overcome heaven by prayer, have declared we would not let Jehovah himself go except he should bless us. We have, and we say it without blasphemy, moved the arm that moves the world. We have brought down upon us the eyes that look upon the universe. All this we have done, not by our own strength, but by the might and by the power of the Spirit; and seeing he has so sweetly enabled us, though we have so often forgotten to thank him; seeing that he has so graciously assisted us, though we have often taken all the glory to ourselves instead of giving it to him, must we not admire his love, and must it not be a fearful sin indeed to grieve the Holy Spirit by whom we are sealed?

Oh, my friends, when I think how often you and I have let the devil in, I wonder the Spirit has not withdrawn from us. The final perseverance of the saints is one of the greatest miracles on record; in fact, it is the sum total of miracles. The perseverance of a saint for a single day is a multitude of miracles of mercy. When you consider that the Spirit is of purer eyes than to behold iniquity, and yet he dwells in the heart where sin often intrudes, a heart out of which come blasphemies, and murders, and all manner of evil thoughts, what if sometimes he is grieved, and retires and leaves us to ourselves for a season? It is a marvel that he is there at all, for he must be daily grieved with these evil guests, these false traitors, these base intruders who thrust themselves into that little temple which he had honored with his presence, the temple of the heart of man.

I am afraid, dear friends, we are too much in the habit of talking about the love of Jesus, without thinking about the love of the Holy Spirit. Now I would not wish to exalt one person of the Trinity above another, but I do feel this, that because Jesus Christ was a man, bone of our bone, and flesh of our flesh, and therefore there was something tangible in him that can be seen with the eyes, and handled with the hands, therefore we more readily think of him, and fix our love on him, than we do on the Spirit. But why should it be? Let us love Jesus with all our hearts, and let us love the Holy Spirit too. Let us have songs for him, gratitude for him. We do not forget Christ's cross; let us not forget the Spirit's work. We do not forget what Jesus has done for us; let us always remember what the Spirit does in us. Why, you talk of the love, and grace, and tenderness, and faithfulness of Christ; why do you not say the same of the Spirit? Was ever love like his, that he should visit us? Was ever mercy like his, that he should bear with our ill manners, though constantly repeated by us? Was ever faithfulness like his, that multitudes of sins cannot drive him away? Was ever power like his, that overcometh all our iniquities, and yet leads us safely on, though hosts of foes within and without would rob us of our Christian life?

> Oh, the love of the Spirit I sing,
> By whom is redemption applied.
> And unto his name be glory for ever and ever.

2. It is by the Holy Spirit that we are sealed.

This brings me to my second point. Here we have another reason why we should not grieve the Spirit. It is by the Holy Spirit that we are sealed. "By whom we are sealed unto the day of redemption." The Spirit himself is expressed as a seal, even as he himself is directly said to be the pledge of our inheritance. The sealing, I think, has a threefold meaning.

(a) A sealing of attestation

It is a sealing of attestation or confirmation. I want to know whether I am truly a child of God. The Spirit itself also bears witness with my spirit that I am born of God. I have the writings, the title-deeds of the inheritance that is to come—I want to know whether those are valid, whether they are true, or whether they are mere counterfeits written out by that old scribe of hell, Master Presumption and Carnal Security. How am I to know? I look for the seal. After we have believed on the Son of God, the Father seals us as his children, by the gift of the Holy Spirit. "Now he which hath anointed us is God, who also hath sealed us, and given the earnest of the Spirit in our hearts." No faith is genuine which does not bear the seal of the Spirit. No love, no hope can ever save us, unless it is sealed with the Spirit of God, for whatever does not have the Spirit of God on it is spurious. Faith that is unsealed may be a poison, it may be presumption; but faith that is sealed by the Spirit is true, real, genuine faith. Never be content, my dear hearers, unless you are sealed, unless you are sure, by the inner witness and testimony of the Holy Spirit, that you have been born again to a living hope by the resurrection of Jesus Christ from the dead. It is possible for a person to know infallibly that he is certain of heaven. He may not only hope so, but he may know it beyond a doubt, and he may know it in this way: by being able with the eye of faith to see the seal, the broad stamp of the Holy Spirit set on his own character and experience. It is a seal of attestation.

(b) A sealing of appropriation

In the next place, it is a sealing of appropriation. When people put their mark on an article, it is to show that it is their own. The farmer brands his tools so that they may not be stolen. They are his. The shepherd marks his sheep that they may be recognized as belonging to his flock. The king himself puts his broad arrow on everything that is his property. So the Holy Spirit puts the broad arm of God on the hearts of all his people. He seals us. "Thou shalt be mine," saith the Lord, "in the day when I make up my jewels." And then the Spirit puts God's seal on us to signify that we are God's reserved inheritance—his special people, the portion in which his soul delights.

c) A sealing of preservation

But, again, by sealing is meant preservation. People seal up what they want to preserve, and when a document is sealed it becomes valid henceforth. Now, it is by the Spirit of God that the Christian is sealed, that he is kept, he is preserved, sealed unto the day of redemption—sealed until Christ comes fully to redeem the bodies of his saints by raising them from the dead, and fully to redeem the world by purging it from sin, and making it a kingdom unto himself in righteousness. We shall hold on our way; we shall be saved. The chosen seed cannot be lost, they must be brought home at last, but how? By the sealing of the Spirit. Apart from that they perish; they are undone. When the last general fire is alight, everything that has not been sealed by the Spirit will be burned up. But the people who have the seal on their forehead will be preserved. They shall be safe, "amid the wreck of matter, and the crash of worlds." Their spirits, mounting above the flames, shall dwell with Christ eternally, and with that same seal on their forehead on Mount Zion, they shall sing the everlasting song of gratitude and praise. I say this is the second reason why we should love the Spirit and why we should not grieve him.

3. The grieving of the Spirit.

I come now to the third part of my discourse, namely, the grieving of the Spirit. How may we grieve him? What will be the sad result of grieving him? If we have grieved him, how may we bring him back again? How may we grieve the Spirit? I am now, please note, speaking about those who love the Lord Jesus Christ. The Spirit of God is in your heart, and it is very, very easy indeed to grieve him. Sin is as easy as it is wicked. You may grieve him by impure thoughts. He cannot bear sin. If you indulge in lascivious expressions, or if even you allow imagination to dwell on any lascivious act, or if your heart goes after covetousness, if you set your heart on anything that is evil, the Spirit of God will be grieved, for thus I hear him speaking of himself. "I love this man, I want to have his heart, and yet he is entertaining these filthy lusts. His thoughts, instead of running after me, and after Christ, and after the Father, are running after the temptations that are in the world through lust." And then his Spirit is grieved. He sorrows in his soul because he knows what sorrow these things must bring to our souls.

We grieve him even more if we indulge in outward acts of sin. Then he is sometimes so grieved that he takes his flight for a season, for the dove will not dwell in our hearts if we take loathsome carrion in there. The dove is a clean being, and we must not strew the place which the dove frequents with filth and mire; if we do he will fly elsewhere. If we commit sin, if we openly bring disgrace on our religion, if we tempt others to sin by our example, it is not long before the Holy Spirit will begin to grieve.

Again, if we neglect prayer, if our closet door is cobwebbed, if we forget to read the Scriptures, if the pages of our Bible are almost stuck together through neglect, if we never seek to do any good in the world, if we live merely for ourselves and not for Christ, then the Holy Spirit will be grieved, for he says, "They have forsaken me, they have left the fountain of waters, they have hewn unto themselves broken cisterns." I think I now see the Spirit of God grieving, when you are sitting down to read a novel and there is your Bible unread. Perhaps you take down some travel book, and you forget that you have got a more precious book of travels in the Acts of the Apostles, and in the story of your blessed Lord and Master. You have no time for prayer, but the Spirit sees you very active about worldly things, and having many hours to spare for relaxation and amusement.

And then he is grieved because he sees that you love worldly things more than you love him. His spirit is grieved within him; take care that he does not go away from you, for it will be a pitiful thing for you if he leaves you to yourself. Again, ingratitude tends to grieve him. Nothing cuts a person to the heart more than, after having done his utmost for another, he turns round and repays him with ingratitude and insult. If we do not want to be thanked, at least we do love to know that there is thankfulness in the heart on which we have conferred a boon, and when the Holy Spirit looks into our soul and sees little love for Christ, no gratitude towards him for all he has done for us, then he is grieved.

Again, the Holy Spirit is exceedingly grieved by our unbelief. When we distrust the promise he has given and applied, when we doubt the power or the affection of our blessed Lord, then the Spirit says within himself: "They doubt my faithfulness; they distrust my power; they say Jesus is not able to save unto the uttermost." Thus the Spirit is grieved again. Oh, I wish the Spirit had an advocate here this morning that could speak in better terms than I can. I have a theme that overwhelms me, I seem to grieve for him; but I cannot make you grieve, nor fully speak about how I feel. In my own soul I keep saying, "Oh, this is just what you have done—you have grieved him." Let me make a full and frank confession even before you all. I know that too often, I as well as you have grieved the Holy Spirit. Much within us has made that sacred dove mourn, and the wonder is that he has not taken his flight from us and left us completely to ourselves.

Now suppose the Holy Spirit is grieved, what is the effect produced in us? When the Spirit is grieved, he bears with us to start with. He is grieved again and again, and again and again, and still he bears with it all. But at last, the grief becomes so excessive that he says, "I will suspend my work; I will go; I will leave life behind me, but my own actual presence I will take away." And when the Spirit of God goes away from the soul and suspends all his work, what a miserable state we are in. He suspends his work; we read the Word, we cannot understand it; we go to our commentaries, they cannot tell us the meaning; we fall on our knees and ask to be taught, but we receive no answer, we learn nothing. He suspends his comfort; we used to dance, like David before the ark, and now we sit like Job in the ash-pit, and scrape our ulcers with a potsherd. There was a time when his candle shone around us, but now he is gone; he has left us in the blackness and darkness. Now, he takes from us all spiritual power. Once we could do all things; now we can do nothing. We could slay the Philistines, and lay them heap upon heap, but now Delilah can deceive us, and our eyes are put out and we are made to grind at the mill. We go preaching, and there is no pleasure in preaching, and no good follows it. We go distributing tracts, and to our Sunday school, and we may as well have stayed at home. The machinery is there, but there is no love. There is the intention to do good, or perhaps not even that, but alas, there is no power to accomplish the intention. The Lord has withdrawn himself, his light, his joy, his comfort, his spiritual power, all are gone.

Then all our graces flag. Our graces are much like the hydrangea flower. When it has plenty of water it blooms, but as soon as moisture fails, the leaves drop down at once. And so when the Spirit goes away, faith shuts up its flowers; no perfume is exhaled. Then the fruit of our love begins to rot and drops from the tree; then the sweet buds of our hope become frostbitten, and they die. Oh, what a sad thing it is to lose the Spirit. Have you never, my brethren, been on your knees and have been conscious that the Spirit of God was not with you, and what awful work it has been to groan, and cry, and sigh, and yet go away again, and no light to shine on the promises, not so much as a ray of light through the chink of the dungeon? All forsaken, forgotten, and forlorn, you are almost driven to despair. You sing with Cowper:

What peaceful hours I once enjoyed,
How sweet their memory still!
But they have left an aching void,
The world can never fill.

Return, thou sacred dove, return,
Sweet messenger of rest,
I hate the sins that made Thee mourn,
And drove Thee from my breast.

The dearest idol I have known,
Whate'er that idol be,
Help me to tear it from its throne,
And worship only Thee.

Ah, sad enough it is to have the Spirit taken away from us. But, my brethren, I am about to say something with the utmost charity which, perhaps, may look severe, but, nevertheless, I must say it. The churches of the present day are very much in the position of those who have grieved the Spirit of God; for the Spirit deals with churches just as it deals with individuals. In recent years how little has God wrought in the middle of his churches! Throughout England, at least some four or five years ago, an almost universal torpor had fallen on the visible body of Christ. There was a little action, but it was spasmodic; there was not real vitality. Oh, how few sinners were brought to Christ, how empty had our places of worship become; our prayer-meetings were dwindling to nothing, and our church meetings were mere matters of farce. You know very well that this is true of many London churches today, and some people do not mourn over this. They go up to their usual place, and the minister prays, and the people either sleep with their eyes or else with their hearts, and they go out, and there is never a soul saved. The pool of baptism is seldom stirred; but the saddest part of all is this: the churches are willing to have it so. They are not earnest to get a revival of religion. We have been doing something, the church at large has been doing something. I will not just now put my finger on what the sin is, but there has been something done which has driven the Spirit of God from us. He is grieved, and he is gone.

He is present with us here, I thank his name, he is still visible in our midst. He has not left us. Though we have been as unworthy as others, yet has he given us a long outpouring of his presence. These five years or more, we have had a revival which is not to be exceeded by any revival upon the face of the earth. Without cries and shoutings, without fallings down or swooning, steadily God adds to this church numbers upon numbers, so that your minister's heart is ready to break with the very joy when he thinks how manifestly the Spirit of God is with us.

But, brethren, we must not be content with this; we want to see the Spirit poured out on all churches. Look at the great gatherings that there were in St. Paul's, and Westminster Abbey, and Exeter Hall, and other places. How was it that no good was done, or so very little? I have watched with anxious eye, and I have never from that day forth heard but of one conversion, and that in St. James' Hall, from all these services. Strange it seems. The blessing may have come in larger measure than we know, but not in so large a measure as we might have expected, if the Spirit of God had been present with all the ministers. Oh, would that we may live to see greater things than we have ever seen yet. Go home to your houses, humble yourselves before God, you members of

Christ's church, and cry aloud that he will visit his church, and that he will open the windows of heaven and pour out his grace on his thirsty hill of Zion, that nations may be born in a day, that sinners may be saved in their thousands—that Zion may go into labor and bear many children.

Oh, there are signs and tokens of a coming revival. We have heard recently of a good work among the Ragged school boys of St. Giles', and our soul has been glad on account of that; and the news from Ireland comes to us like good tidings. Let us cry aloud to the Holy Spirit, who is certainly grieved with his church, and let us purge our churches of everything that is contrary to his Word and to sound doctrine, and then the Spirit will return, and his power will be manifest.

Conclusion

And now there may be some present who have lost the visible presence of Christ with you; who have in fact so grieved the Spirit that he has gone. It is a mercy for you to know that the Spirit of God never leaves his people finally; he leaves them for chastisement, but not for damnation. He sometimes leaves them that they may get good by knowing their weakness, but he will not leave them finally to perish. Are you in a state of backsliding and coldness? Christian friend, do not stay a moment longer in this dangerous condition. Do not be at ease for a single second that the Holy Spirit is not with you. I plead with you to use every means through which that Spirit may be brought back to you.

Once more, let me tell you clearly what these means are. Search out for the sin that has grieved the Spirit, give it up, put that sin to death at once; repent with tears and sighs; continue in prayer, and never rest satisfied until the Holy Spirit has returned to you. Attend an earnest ministry, get much with earnest saints, but above all, be much in prayer to God, and let your daily cry be, "Return, return, O Holy Spirit return, and live in my soul."

Oh, I plead with you not to be content until that prayer is heard, for you have become weak as water, and faint and empty while the Spirit has been away from you. Oh, it may be there are some here today with whom the Spirit has been striving during the past week. Oh yield to him, resist him not; grieve him not, but yield to him. Is he saying to you now, "Turn to Christ"? Listen to him, obey him, he moves you. Oh, I beseech you, do not despise him. Have you resisted him many times? Then take care you do not again, for there may come a last time when the Spirit may say, "I will go unto my rest, I will not return to him, the ground is accursed, it shall be given up to barrenness." Oh, hear the word of the gospel, before you separate, for the Spirit speaks effectively to you now in this short sentence: "Repent and be converted every one of you, that your sins may be blotted out when the times of refreshing shall come from the presence of the Lord." Also, take this solemn sentence to heart: "He that believeth in the Lord Jesus, and is baptized, shall be saved; but he that believeth not shall be damned." May the Lord grant that we may not grieve the Holy Spirit. Amen.

CHAPTER SIX

Awareness of Sin in Revival

> *Therefore let all the house of Israel know
> assuredly, that God hath made that same Jesus,
> whom ye have crucified, both Lord and Christ. Now
> when they heard this, they were pricked in their
> heart, and said unto Peter and to the rest of the
> apostles, Men and brethren, what shall we do?*
> ACTS 2:36-37

This was the first public preaching of the gospel after our Lord was taken up into glory. It was thus a very memorable sermon, a kind of firstfruits of the great harvest of gospel testimony. It is very encouraging to those who are engaged in preaching that the first sermon should have been so successful. Three thousand made up a grand take of fish at that first cast of the net. We are serving a great and growing cause in the way chosen by God, and we hope in the future to see still greater results produced by that same undying and unchanging power which helped Peter to preach such a heart-piercing sermon.

Peter's discourse was not remarkable for any special display of rhetoric. He did not use words of human wisdom or eloquence. It was not an oration, but it was a heart-moving argument, entreaty, and exhortation. He gave his hearers a simple, well-reasoned, scriptural discourse, sustained by the facts of experience; and every passage of it pointed to the Lord Jesus. It was in these respects a model of what a sermon ought to be as to its contents. His plea was personally addressed to the people who stood before him, and it had a practical and pressing relation to them and to their conduct. It was plain, practical, personal, and persuasive; and in this it was a model of what a sermon ought to be in its aim and style.

Yet Peter could not have spoken in any other way under the impression of the divine Spirit: his speech was as the oracles of God, a true product of a divine inspiration. Under the circumstances, any other kind of address would have been sadly out of place. A flashy, dazzling oration would have been a piece of horrible irreverence to the Holy Spirit; and Peter would have been guilty of the blood of souls if he had attempted it. In sober earnestness he kept to the plain facts of the case, setting them in the light of God's Word; and then with all his might he pressed home the truth on those for whose salvation he was laboring.

May it always be the preacher's one desire to win men and women to repentance towards God and faith in our Lord Jesus Christ. May no minister wish to be admired, but may he long that his Lord and Master may be sought after! Oh that we could so preach that our hearers should be at once pricked in their hearts, and so be led at once to believe in our Lord Jesus, and immediately to come forward and confess their faith in his name.

We must not forget, however, to trace the special success of the sermon on the day of Pentecost to the outpouring of the Holy Spirit, in which Peter had shared. This it is which is the making of the preacher. Immersed in the Holy Spirit, the preacher will think rightly, and speak wisely; his word will be with power to those who hear. We must not forget, also, that there had been a long season of earnest, united, believing prayer on the part of the whole church. Peter was not alone: he was the voice of a praying company, and the believers had been with one accord in one place crying for a blessing; and thus not only was the Spirit resting on the preacher, but on all who were with him. What a difference it makes to a preacher of the gospel, when all his comrades are as much anointed by the Spirit as himself. His power is enhanced a hundredfold. We will rarely see the very greatest wonders wrought when the preacher stands by himself; but when Peter is described as standing up "with the eleven," then there is a twelve-man ministry concentrated in one person. And when the inner circle is further sustained by a company of men and women who have entered into the same truth, and are of one heart and one soul, then the power is increased beyond measure.

A lonely ministry may sometimes effect great things, as Jonah did in Nineveh; but if we look for the greatest and most desirable result of all, it must come from one who is not alone, but is the mouthpiece of many. Peter had the one hundred twenty registered brethren for a loving bodyguard, and this tended to make him strong for his Lord. How greatly I value the loving cooperation of the friends around me. I have no words to express my gratitude to God for the army of true men and women who surround me with their love, and support me with their faith. I pray you, never cease to sustain me by your prayers, your sympathy, your cooperation, until some other preacher shall take my place when increasing years shall warn me to step aside.

Yet much responsibility must rest with the preacher himself;

and there was much about Peter's own self that is well worth imitation. The sermon was born of the occasion, and it used the event of the hour as God intended it to be used. Peter aired no theories, but went on firm ground, stepping from one fact to another fact, from Scripture to Scripture, from plain truth to plain truth. He was patient at the beginning, used arguments all the way through, and had a conclusion. He fought his way through the doubts and prejudices of his hearers. All along he spoke very boldly, without compromising the truth—"Ye with wicked hands have crucified and slain him whom God has highly exalted." Peter bravely accused them of murdering the Lord of glory, doing his duty in the sight of God, and for the good of their souls, with great firmness and fearlessness.

Yet there is great tenderness in his discourse. Impulsive and hotheaded Peter, who, a little before, had drawn his sword to fight for his Lord, does not, in this instance, use a harsh word. He speaks with great gentleness and meekness of spirit, using words which indicate a desire to conciliate and then to convince. Peter was gentle in his manner, but forceful in his matter. This art he had learned from his Lord; and we will never have masterpreachers among us until we see men who have been with Jesus and have learned from him. Oh, that we could become partakers of our Lord's spirit, and echoes of his tone! Then may we hope to attain the Pentecostal results when we have preachers like Peter, surrounded by a band of earnest witnesses, and all baptized with the Holy Spirit and with fire.

When we follow Peter's argument, we will not be surprised that his hearers were pricked to the heart. We ascribe that deep pricking of the conscience to the Spirit of God; and yet it was a very reasonable thing that it should be so. When it was clearly shown that they had really crucified the Messiah, the great hope of their nation, it was not surprising that they should be smitten with horror. But for the result of our ministry we depend wholly on the Spirit of God, yet we must adapt our discourse so that we achieve our aim; or, rather, we must leave ourselves in the Spirit's hand about the sermon itself as well as about its results. The Holy Spirit uses means which are adapted to a specific end. Because, dear Christian friends, I desire, above everything else, that many in this congregation are pricked in their hearts, I have taken this concluding part of Peter's sermon to be my text this morning. Yet my trust is not in the Word itself, but in the quickening Spirit who works through it. May the Spirit of God use the rapier of his Word to pierce the hearts of my hearers!

First, note that Peter speaks to his hearers about their evil behavior towards the Lord Jesus; and, second, he declares to them the exaltation that God had bestowed on him. Third, we will note the result of knowing this great fact—"Let all the house of Israel know assuredly that God hath made that same Jesus, whom ye have crucified, both Lord and Christ."

1. Their evil behavior towards the Lord Jesus.

First, then, Peter emphasized tenderly, but plainly, their evil behavior towards the Lord Jesus. "He came unto his own, and his own received him not." As a nation, Israel had rejected him whom God had sent. The inhabitants of Jerusalem had gone further, and had consented to his death. Indeed, they had even clamored for it, crying, "Crucify him, crucify him." Peter reminded them that they were guilty of this. It is well when a sense of guilt compels a person to stand silent under God's rebuke. Then we have hope that we can receive his pardon.

(a) Blaspheming the name of Jesus

We are not in Jerusalem, and our Lord's death happened 1,800 years ago, so we need not dwell on the sins of those who have long been dead. It will be better for us if we consider how far we have been guilty of similar sins against the Lord Jesus Christ. Let us each look to ourselves. I may be addressing some today who have blasphemed the name of the Lord Jesus. You may not have been guilty of the vulgar language of blasphemy, but there is a politer way of committing the same crime. Some, with their elaborate criticisms of Christianity, wound it far more seriously than atheists with their profanities. Denying the atonement or teaching it as something other than a substitutionary sacrifice is to do away with the heart and soul of the Redeemer's work. The cross is still a stone of stumbling and a rock of offense. People do not now accept the words of the Bible as authoritative nor the teaching of the apostles as final; they set themselves up to be teachers of the great Teacher, reformers of the divine gospel. If any present have been guilty of this, may the Holy Spirit convince them of their sin.

(b) Neglecting the Lord Jesus

Much more common, however, is another sin against our Lord Jesus—namely, neglecting him, ignoring his claims, and postponing the day of faith in him. I trust that no one here is willing to die unconverted. Yet you have lived to adulthood, and perhaps to old age, without yielding your hearts to the Lord Jesus, and accepting him as your Savior. To say the very least, this is a very sad piece of neglect. To ignore a person altogether is, in a sense, as far as you are concerned, to kill that person. If you put him out of your reckoning, if you treat him as if he were nothing, you have put your Lord out of existence in reference to yourself. He is dead to you. You have never confessed your sin before him, or sought pardon from his hands, or looked to see if he has borne your sins in his own body on the tree. O soul, this is base neglect—ungrateful contempt! Will you treat your Savior in this way? May this prick you in your heart, and may you cease being so ungrateful.

(c) Rejection of the Lord Jesus

Other people have gone further than this, for they have rejected Christ. Some of you have deliberately rejected Christ almost every Sunday; and especially when the Word of the Lord has been preached with extraordinary power, and you have felt it shake you, as a lion shakes its prey. Thank God you are not beyond feeling yet. You will not always feel as you have felt. The day may come when even God's thunders may not be heard by your deaf ear, and Christ's love will not affect your calloused heart. Woe to the man when his heart is turned to stone. When flesh turns to stone it is a conversion to eternal death. God have mercy on you this morning and prick your heart to embrace Christ with all your heart.

(d) Forsaking of the Lord Jesus

There are a few unhappy people here this morning over whom I grieve greatly because of their wanderings; and yet I am glad that they have not quite forsaken the courts of the Lord's house. They once professed to be Christ's disciples, but they have gone back and walk with him no more. Friend, you are here this morning so that I can remind you of your sin and ask you why you have done this! Were you a hypocrite? If not, why have you turned away? God has exalted to his throne the Savior on whom you have turned your back; have you not acted madly in what you have done? The Most High God is on the side of Jesus, and you are definitely on the other side; is this right, or wise? It is painful for me to speak of these things. I hope that it is far more painful for you to listen to them. Turn, I pray you, from your evil way, and turn to the Lord with your full heart.

2. The exaltation God gave to the Lord Jesus.

After Peter had dwelt on the sin of his hearers in treating the Lord so badly, he declared to them the exaltation bestowed on Christ by God. The great God loved, honored, and exalted that same Jesus whom they had crucified. O my hearers, whatever you may think of the Lord Jesus Christ, God thinks everything of him. To you he may be dead and buried, but God has raised him from the dead. My hearer, whatever you do, you cannot shake the truth of the gospel, nor rob the Lord Jesus of a single beam of his glory. He lives and reigns, and he will live and reign, whatever becomes of you. You may refuse his salvation, but he is still a Savior, and a great one.

(a) Our Lord enjoys infinite happiness

Let me remind you that when we read of our Lord being at God's right hand we see that he enjoys infinite felicity. At the right hand of God there are pleasures for evermore. He who was the man of sorrows now overflows with gladness. He is full of joy, that joy which he invites his people to share when he says, "Enter thou into the joy of thy Lord."

(b) Our Lord sits in infinite majesty

Moreover, remember that at the right hand of God our Lord sits in infinite majesty. He is the highest in the highest heavens. Do you not hear the song which ascribes to him honor, and glory, and power, and dominion, and might? My faith anticipates the happy day when I shall stand as a courtier in his courts and behold him, the Lamb on the throne reigning over all with every knee in heaven and earth gladly bowing before him.

(c) Our Lord is exalted to the place of power

Nor is this all: for the place at the right hand of God, to which Christ is now exalted, is the place of power. There sits the Mediator, the Son of God, the Man Jesus Christ, while his enemies are being subdued under him. All power is given to him in heaven and earth; he reigns in the three realms of nature, providence, and grace. Yet it is this Christ, this mighty Christ, who is set at nought by some of you, so that you run the risk of perishing because you have no heart for him and his great salvation.

(d) Our Lord is seated as our Judge

Learn, next, that he is at the right hand of Majesty in the heavens, seated as our Judge. If we refuse him as a Savior, we shall not be able to escape from him as Judge in the last great day. If you refuse him, you will have to stand before his bar to answer for it. The most awful sight for the impenitent in the day of judgment will be the face of the Lord Jesus Christ. If you refuse the Lord's Word, you refuse him who speaks from heaven: you refuse not only his words, but himself, and he will be your Judge.

(e) Our Lord is Head over all things in his church

Peter also said that the Lord was greatly exalted in heaven as the Head over all things to his church, for he had that day shed abroad the Holy Spirit. When the Holy Spirit comes, he comes from Christ, and as the witness of his power. He proceeds from the Father and the Son, and he bears witness to both. Christ's power was wonderfully proved when, after he had been only a short while in heaven, he bestowed such gifts on men and women: especially sending the tongues of fire and the rushing mighty wind, which are tokens of the power of the Holy Spirit. He can this morning send salvation to the ends of the earth so that thousands of people believe and live. You must be sure about this, you Gentiles, just as Peter wanted the house of Israel to be certain about it, that "God hath made that same Jesus, whom ye have crucified, both Lord and Christ."

I notice that, at this time, few writers or preachers use the expression "Our Lord Jesus Christ." We have lives of Christ and lives of Jesus, but, brethren, he is the Lord. Jesus is both Lord and Christ: we need to acknowledge his deity, his dominion, and his divine anointing. God has made this same Jesus "both Lord and Christ"; let us worship him as Lord and trust him as Christ.

3. The result of knowing for certain about Christ's death and exaltation

Now I come to my closing point, which is, the result of knowing this assuredly. May I pause here to ask—do you know this for certain? I hope all of you believe that God has made Jesus Christ, the Mediator, as God and man, to be "both Lord and Christ." Manhood and Godhead are in him united in one wonderful Person, and this Person is "both Lord and Christ." Do you believe with certainty that the Man of Nazareth, who died on Calvary, is today both Lord and Christ. If you do now believe this, what are your feelings as you review your past bad behavior towards Christ?

(a) Peter's hearers felt a mortal sting

Observe, that as the result of Peter's sermon, his hearers felt a mortal sting. "They were pricked to the heart." The truth had pierced their souls. When a person finds out that he has done some terrible wrong to someone who loves him, he grows sick at heart and views his own behavior with abhorrence.

There is a story about Llewellyn and his faithful dog. The prince came back from the hunt, and missed his infant child, but saw marks of blood everywhere. Suspecting his dog Gelert of having killed the child, he drove his sword into his faithful hound, which had been bravely defending his child against a huge wolf, which lay there, all torn and dead, "tremendous still in death." Yes, he had killed the faithful creature which had preserved his child. Poor Gelert's dying yell pierced the prince to the heart; and well it might. If such emotions rightly arise when we discover that we have, in error, been ungenerous and cruel to a dog, how ought we to feel towards the Lord Jesus, who laid down his life that we, who were his enemies, might live?

I recall an awfully tragic story about an evil couple, who kept an inn of base repute. A young man called one night to stay there. They noticed that he had gold in his purse, and they murdered him in the night. It was their own son who had come back to make their old age happy and wanted to see if his parents would remember him. Oh, the bitterness of their crying when they discovered that through their greed for gold they had murdered their own son!

Take out of such amazing grief its better part and then add to it a spiritual conviction of the sin of evil—entreating the Son of God, the perfect One, the Lover of our souls, and you come close to the meaning of being "pricked to the heart." Oh, to think that we should despise him who loved us and gave himself for us and should rebel against him who bought us with his own blood while we were his enemies. I would to God everyone here, who has not come to Christ, would feel a sting in his conscience now; and would mourn that he has done this exceeding evil thing against the ever-blessed Son of God, who became man, and died for love of guilty people.

(b) They were stirred to love Christ

When we read "they were pricked in their heart," it means that they felt a movement of love towards Christ—a relenting of heart, a stirring of emotion towards him. They said to themselves, "Have we treated him like this? What can we do to show our horror of our own conduct?" They were not only convinced about their fault so that they grieved over it, but their desires and affections went out towards the offended one, and they cried, "What shall we do? Is there any way of undoing this ill towards him whom we now love?" I would that you all came to this point. I wish you knew the meaning of Newton's hymn:

> I saw One hanging on a tree,
> In agonies and blood,
> Who fix'd His languid eyes on me,
> As near His cross I stood.
>
> Sure never till my latest breath
> Can I forget that look;
> It seem'd to charge me with His death,
> Though not a word He spoke.

My conscience felt and own'd the guilt,
And plunged me in despair;
I saw my sins His blood had spilt,
And help'd to nail Him there.

Alas! I knew not what I did;
But now my tears are vain;
Where shall my trembling soul be hid?
For I the Lord have slain.

Let us tearfully enquire how we can end our opposition and prove ourselves to be his friends and humble servants.

(c) They showed obedient faith

As a result of Peter's sermon, preached in the power of the Holy Spirit, these people showed obedient faith. They were roused to action, and they said, "Men and brethren, what shall we do?" When Peter said, "Repent," they did indeed repent. Then Peter said, "Be baptized every one of you in the name of Jesus Christ for the remission of sins." Take the open and decisive step; stand up as believers in Jesus, and confess him by that outward and visible sign which he has ordained.

O my hearers, to what a place have I brought you now! If indeed the Holy Spirit has helped you to follow my sermon, see where we have climbed. However dark your crime, however vile your character, if you have seen the wrong that you have done, if you have repented of having done it because you see that you have sinned against your loving Lord, and if you will now come to him repenting and believing, and will confess him in baptism; then you have full remission and you will be partakers of the gifts and graces of the Holy Spirit, and you will be chosen witnesses for the Christ whom God has raised from the dead.

May God write out this old, old story on your hearts! Oh, that he would issue a new edition of his gospel of love, printed on your hearts! Every person's conversion is a freshly printed copy of the poem of salvation. May the Lord issue you hot from the press this morning, a living letter to be known and read by everyone; and especially to be read by your children at home, and your neighbors in the same street. The Lord grant that hearts may be pricked by this sermon, for his name's sake. Amen.

CHAPTER SEVEN

Mission in Times of Revival

The Holy Spirit's threefold conviction of people

*And when he is come, he will reprove the world of
sin, and of righteousness, and of judgment: of sin,
because they believe not on me; of righteousness,
because I go to my Father, and ye see me no more; of
judgment, because the prince of this world is judged.*
JOHN 16:8-11

The apostles had a stern task in front of them. They were to
go unto all nations and proclaim the gospel to every creature,
beginning at Jerusalem. Remember that only two or three
years before they were simple fishermen—men of little or no
education, men of no rank or standing. At best they were but
Jews, and that nation was everywhere despised, and these
peasants were not even men of repute among their own
nation. Yet these men were to turn the world upside down.
They were told by their Lord that they would be brought
before rulers and kings for his sake, and that they would be
persecuted wherever they went. They were to proclaim the
gospel in the teeth of the imperial power of Rome, and the
ancient wisdom of Greece, and the fierce cruelties of barbaric

lands, and to set up the kingdom of peace and righteousness.

At the very moment when they were about to receive their commission, they were also to lose the bodily presence of their great Leader. While he was with them they had felt no fear. But now that he was to leave this world and go to the Father they would be deprived of their fortress and high tower; they would be like orphans, or, at best, as soldiers without a general. Here was a sad case. Work given, and power withdrawn: a battle beginning, and the conquering captain leaving.

How happy it was for these disciples that our blessed Lord could tell them that his going away would be to their advantage and not to their disadvantage. For after he left them, the Spirit of God would come to be an Advocate for them and with them, and by his power they would be able to silence all their enemies and achieve their mission.

The Holy Spirit was to be their Comforter, that they might not be afraid; and their Advocate, that they might not be baffled. When they spoke, there would be a power within them suggesting their words, a power with those words convincing their hearers, and a power in their hearers causing the word spoken to abide in their memories: that power would be divine, the power of the Holy Spirit, who is one God with the Father and the Son.

It is one thing for men to speak and quite another thing for God to speak through men. The work of proclaiming the gospel to the world was far too great for the twelve; but it was by no means too great for the Spirit of God. Who can limit his power? Is anything too hard for the Lord? The Holy Spirit being their helper, these feeble men were equal to the task which God had committed to their trust. The presence of the Holy Spirit was better for them than the bodily presence of the

Lord Jesus. The Lord Jesus could only have been in one place at a time in the body, but the Holy Spirit could be everywhere. The sight of Jesus would appeal to the senses, but the power of the Holy Spirit touched the heart and brought spiritual life and saving faith. Thus, by his own withdrawal and the sending of the Spirit, our Lord furnished his servants for the conflict.

We will observe what the Holy Spirit did as an Advocate. To my mind this passage is a compendium of all the work of the Spirit of God. In it was seen, first, the Spirit of God going with the preaching of the gospel to reprove people of their sin, and so to abash them in the presence of the preacher of righteousness; to convince people of sin, and so to lead them to repentance towards God and faith in our Lord Jesus Christ; and, third, the ultimate result of the Holy Spirit's work will be to convict people of being guilty of the grossest sin, of having opposed the most perfect righteousness. We shall try to see the meaning of the passage through these three windows.

1. To reprove people.

First, we believe that a promise is made here to Christ's servants, that when they go and preach the gospel the Holy Spirit will be with them to reprove people. By this is meant not so much to save them as to silence them. When Christ's minister stands up to plead his Master's cause, another Advocate appears in court, whose pleadings would make it hard for men to resist the truth.

(a) About sin

Observe how this reproof was given with regard to sin. On the day of Pentecost the disciples spoke in different tongues, as the Spirit gave them utterance. People from all countries under heaven heard themselves spoken to in their native languages.

When Peter stood up to preach and told the Jews that they had crucified the Holy One, the signs and wonders wrought by the Spirit in the name of Jesus were a witness which they could not refute. The fact that the Spirit of God had given to these uneducated men the gift of tongues was evidence that Jesus of Nazareth, of whom they spoke, was no impostor.

The Lord Jesus Christ had promised the outpouring of the Spirit. When, therefore, that mark of the true Messiah rested on Jesus of Nazareth by the coming of the Holy Spirit and the working of miracles, people were reproved for having refused to believe in Jesus. The evidence was brought home to them that they had with wicked hands crucified the Lord of glory, and so they stood reproved.

All the subsequent miracles went to prove the same thing; for when the apostles wrought miracles the world was reproved of sin because it believed not on Christ. It was not that a few disciples testified to the sin of the race, but the Holy Spirit himself made men tremble as by his deeds of power he bore witness to the Lord Jesus. Do you not see the wonderful power with which the first disciples were thus armed? It needed all the willfulness of that stiff-necked generation to resist the Holy Spirit and refuse to bow before him whom they had pierced.

(b) About righteousness

Do you not see, too, dear friends, how the working of the Holy Spirit with the apostles and their immediate followers was a great rebuke to the world about righteousness? Jesus was gone. His divine example no longer stood out like a clear light reproving the darkness, but the Holy Spirit attested that righteousness and compelled them to feel that Jesus was the Holy One and that his cause was righteous. The teaching of the apostles, sealed by the Holy Spirit, made the world see what righteousness was as they had never seen it before.

The world had then sunk into the depths of vice, and even its good men were loathsome; but now another kind of righteousness was seen in the teachings of the Lord Jesus, and the Spirit came to set the seal of divine approval on it. So if people continued to sin it would be against light and knowledge, for they knew what righteousness was. God was with the preachers of a new righteousness, and by various signs and wonders he attested the cause of the gospel. Today, we are the covenanted servants of a Lord whose righteousness was declared among men by the personal witness of God the Holy Spirit.

(c) About judgment

Then, too, they felt that a judgment had come; that somehow the life and the death of Jesus of Nazareth had made a crisis in the world's history and condemned the way of the ungodly. The thought flashed on humanity, more clearly than it had ever done before, that there would be a day of judgment. People heard and felt the truth of the warning that God would judge the world at the last by the man Christ Jesus. The Holy Spirit had reproved men and women through the prospect of judgment.

The Holy Spirit attested the life of Christ, the teaching of the apostles, and all the great truths that were contained therein, by what he did through miracles, and what he did in the way of enlightening, impressing, and subduing human hearts. From now on humankind is accused and rebuked by the great Advocate; and all who remain opposed to the Lord Jesus defy the clearest evidences for his mission. The person who rejects human testimony when it is true is foolish; but he who despises the witness of the Holy Spirit is profane, for he gives the lie to the Spirit of truth. Let him take care in case he sins against the Holy Spirit and can never be forgiven.

So much for this part of the text. Let us move on to that part of the text which is of more interest to you.

2. To convince people

The Holy Spirit was to go with the preaching of the word to convince people of three great truths. This was to be a saving word: they are to be so convinced as to repent of sin, to accept righteousness, and to yield themselves to the judgment of the Lord. Here is a map of the work of the Spirit on the hearts of those who are ordained to eternal life. Those three effects are all necessary, and each one is most important for true conversion.

(a) To convince people about sin

First, the Holy Spirit came to convince people about sin. The fashionable theology is—"Convince people about the goodness of God: show them the universal fatherhood and assure them of unlimited mercy." But the way of the Spirit of God is very different. He comes to convince people about sin, to make them feel that they are guilty, very guilty—so guilty that they are lost, and ruined, and undone. The Holy Spirit comes to remind them not only of God's loveliness, but of their own unloveliness. The Holy Spirit does not come to make sinners comfortable in their sins, but to make them grieve over their sins.

Flowers fill the fields when the grass is green. But, then, a burning wind comes from the desert, and the grass withers and the flowers fall down. What makes the beauty and excellence of human righteousness like green grass? Isaiah says it is "because the Spirit of the Lord bloweth upon it." There is a withering work of the Spirit of God which we must experience or we will never know his quickening and restoring power. This withering is a most necessary experience and just now needs to be greatly insisted on. Today we have so many built up who were never pulled down; so many filled who were never emptied; so many exalted who were never humbled; that I more earnestly remind you that the Holy Spirit must convince us of sin or we cannot be saved.

Note that the Spirit of God comes to convince people about sin, because they will never be convinced about sin apart from his divine advocacy. A natural conscience touched by the Spirit of God may do a good deal to reveal a person's faults; it may thus make him uneasy, and may bring about a reformation of life; but it is only the Spirit of God that will so convince a person about sin that it results in repentance, self-despair, and faith in Jesus. It is not easy, brethren, to explain this. But this I know, that the extent of sin is never known until the Spirit of God reveals the secret rooms of the heart's abominations. We do a thousand things that we do not know to be sin until the Spirit of God enlightens us and pleads the cause of holiness in us. The fact that we not only sin, but are by nature sinful, is one which our pride kicks against, and we will not learn about it until the Spirit of God teaches it to us. Nobody knows about the sinfulness of sin until the light of the Holy Spirit falls on the dark mass.

The Holy Spirit dwells on one point in particular: "of sin, because they believe not on me." No one sees the sin of unbelief except by the Spirit's light. People think, "Unbelief is a matter of very little consequence; I can set that right at any time." But the Holy Spirit makes a person see that not to believe in Christ is the crowning, damning sin.

(b) To convince people about righteousness

The next work of the Spirit is to convince people about righteousness. In terms of the gospel this means showing them that they have no righteousness of their own and no way of creating righteousness, and that apart from grace they are condemned. Thus, the Holy Spirit leads them to value the righteousness of God which is on all who believe, this righteousness which covers sin and makes people acceptable with God.

Lend me your ears a moment while I draw your attention to a great wonder. Among men, if a person is convicted of wrongdoing, the next step is judgment. A young man is caught embezzling money. He is taken to court and convicted of the crime and found guilty. What follows next? Why, judgment is pronounced and he must bear the penalty. But note how our gracious God inserts an additional process. He does convict of sin, so you would expect the next step to be judgment; but no, the Lord introduces a hitherto unknown middle term as he convinces about "righteousness." Be amazed at this. The Lord takes a person, even when he is sinful and conscious of that sin, and makes him righteous on the spot by putting away his sin and justifying him by the righteousness of faith, a righteousness which comes to him by the worthiness of another who has bought a righteousness for him. Can that be? Brethren, this seems to be a thing so impossible that it needs the Spirit of God to convince people about it.

All my labors of preaching are in vain until the Spirit makes God's righteousness plain. Many people hear the good news, but they do not receive the truth, for they are not convinced about it. They need to be persuaded about it before they will embrace it, and that kind of persuasion is not in my power.

Did I hear someone say, "I cannot see this way of righteousness"? I reply, "No, and you never will until the Spirit of God convinces you about it."

Dear people of God, pray hard that the Spirit of God may even now convince unbelievers that the only true righteousness for mortal humans is that which comes not by the works of the law, but by the hearing of faith.

(c) To convince people about judgment

But then comes a third point: the Spirit of God is to convince people about judgment. To whom is this judgment committed? "The Father hath committed all judgment unto the Son." The Spirit of God is needed to convince our unbelieving hearts that this is the case.

Let me run over this ground, that we may not overlook anything. Dear friends, those of us who are saved still need the Holy Spirit with us every day to convince us about sin. Good people still do wicked things. May the Holy Spirit continually show us layer after layer of sin, that we may remove it; may he reveal to us rank after rank of sin, that we may conquer all its forces. Whenever our hearts distrust the Lord we grieve his Spirit; hence we always need the Holy Spirit to convince us of this evil and bitter thing, and to lead us to trust God in a childlike way. Oh, convincing Spirit, dwell with me from day to day convincing me of sin, and especially making me feel that the worst of all evils is to question my faithful Friend.

So, also, may you always have the Spirit of God dwelling in you, convincing you of righteousness. "There is therefore now no condemnation to them which are in Christ Jesus." Oh, may the Spirit of God every day convince you of that; and convince you of it on the ground that Jesus is reigning at the Father's right hand. The interest of each believer in his Lord is clear and sure. Jesus is exalted, not for himself alone, but for all who believe in him. May the blessed Spirit fully convince you of this great truth.

And, next, may he convince you about judgment—namely, that you have been judged, and your enemy has been judged and condemned. The day of judgment is not a thing to be dreaded by a believer. We have stood our trial, and have been acquitted. Our representative has borne the penalty of our sin. There is now no curse for us: there can be none: heaven, earth, hell cannot find a curse for those whom God has blessed, since the Lord Jesus "was made a curse for us." May the Spirit of God come on you afresh, my dearly beloved, and make you confident and joyful in him who is the Lord our righteousness, by whom evil has been judged once for all!

3. To convict people.

Last of all, let us read our text, by translating it "convict." "The Spirit of God will convict the world of sin, of righteousness, and of judgment." There is the world. It stands a prisoner at the bar, and the charge is that it is and has been full of sin. Everyone agrees, "He is a villain if ever there was one." Now hear the Spirit of God. The Spirit came into the world to make everyone know that Jesus is the Christ. But what did the wicked world do with Christ? They nailed him to a cross. By this the world is condemned. We need no further evidence. The world is convicted. The world's guilt is proved beyond doubt. The wrath of God abides on it.

What happens after this? The trial is viewed from another point of view. Up to this day the world is trying to defeat God's cause. But the Spirit of God, through his teaching, proves that the gospel is full of righteousness. By sanctifying people through the gospel the Holy Spirit proves that the gospel is righteous. The Holy Spirit makes the world know that Christ is righteous by flashing into its face the fact that Christ has gone—gone up to glory, at the right hand of God—and this could not have happened if he had not been the righteous One.

When the world sees Jesus enthroned, and everyone looks at the Son of Man in the clouds of heaven, what conviction will seize every mind! Then the Spirit of God will make everyone see the judgment. Oh, how the Spirit of God will convict everyone at that last day when they hear the Judge say, "Come, ye blessed of my Father," or "Depart, ye cursed, into everlasting fire."

Christian friends, will you be convinced by the Holy Spirit now, or will you wait till then? Will it be the conviction of grace or the conviction of wrath? The Spirit still bears witness with us who preach the gospel: will you yield to that gospel, and believe it now? Or will you wait until the blaze of the last tremendous day? O Spirit of God, make us sane and wise, for Christ Jesus' sake. Amen.

CHAPTER EIGHT

The Role of Prayer in Revival

*If a son shall ask bread of any of you that is a
father, will he give him a stone? or if he ask a fish,
will he for a fish give him a serpent? or if he shall
ask an egg, will he offer him a scorpion? If ye then,
being evil, know how to give good gifts unto your
children: how much more shall your heavenly
Father give the Holy Spirit to them that ask him?*
LUKE 11:11-13

In this chapter there is an evident progress. It opens by the
disciples asking the Lord to teach them to pray. To that he
gave a full and sufficient reply; he prepared them an outline of
what complete prayer should be. Brethren, we need, some of
us, to begin with asking to be taught to pray. It will be a
blessed sign when it can be said of us, "Behold, he prayeth";
and in the same proportion as we are instructed how to pray
shall we give evidence of more advanced Christian life. He has
most grown in grace who prays best. Depend upon it, the
most acceptable prayer with God is the evidence of a most
accepted state of heart within. Our growth in prayer may be to
us the test of our growth in all other respects. "Lord, teach us

to pray," is a prayer for the young beginner and for the more advanced disciple; it is a suitable petition for us all, for we have none of us yet learned to the full the sacred art of supplication.

Then the chapter proceeds a little further to answer a question: we are shown how to pray, but will God answer us? Is prayer only meant to do good to the suppliant? Does it end with the benefit which it works in us, or does it really affect the heart of God? Do replies actually come from heaven in answer to the entreaties of God's children? The answer is given by our Lord with great clearness. We have a parable to show that as importunity does evidently affect men, so importunity will also gain an answer from God, that he will be pleased to give us what we need if we do but know how, with incessant earnestness, to come again and again to him in prayer. We are assured that asking is attended with receiving, that seeking is attended with finding, that knocking will lead to opening, that it is not a vain thing to pray, that our prayers are not lost on the wind or expended merely on ourselves, but that there is a connection established by divine decree between the prayer that is raised on earth and the mercy that is given forth from heaven.

But since we are such sinful creatures, the chapter proceeds to deal with a grave doubt which may arise in the troubled mind. "It may be God will hear, and as a general rule will make replies in mercy; but I am an undeserving one; if the Lord should be incensed at my prayers and answer me in wrath instead of love, I should deserve it; if after having made my confession, he should deal with me after judging me out of my own mouth, and there and then condemn me, what should I say?" The Savior explicitly answers the question as to whether God will give answers of peace, and will always grant us good things; and he puts it thus to us: when your children ask for good things you grant their requests; you do not mock them by giving them something that may look like what they asked for, but it is only a deception; you never play upon their ignorance and mock their childish confidence by giving them the injurious semblance of what would have been a useful reality. When their prayers are right you answer them. If you then, being evil, fallen creatures, yet answer your children's right and proper prayers, how much more will your heavenly Father answer your fitting prayers and give to you good things? He will not put you off with evil things when you ask for good, but he will grant you in truth the good gifts which you are seeking after.

You will observe that the fear lest God should give something evil when we are seeking something good, is very naturally raised in the heart by a sense of sinfulness, and is increased by the conviction that we should not always be able to judge whether the thing received be good or no good. We tremble lest we should receive from the divine hands what appears to be gracious, and yet may be sent in judgment. But he says, "No, your children trust in their father, and their father never deceives them: you may safely trust your heavenly Father that when you ask a good thing from him, he will most assuredly give you a good thing, and not an evil thing in its place." You are true and kind to your children, much more will God be good towards you. In saying "How much more?" he asks an unanswerable question. As high as God is above us, so high is the certainty that he will give us good things. We feel in our hearts quite certain that God will never mock us and give to us an evil thing when we are seeking a good thing from his hands. By the way, it has been remarked that our Savior's expression here is, "ye being evil"; that expression evidently teaching the doctrine of our fallen condition, the doctrine of human depravity. You, my disciples, you are evil.

You who have children, whether you are upright or otherwise in other people's opinions, you are all evil, and yet, being evil, you still have such affection and judgment that you give your children good gifts; much more shall he who is infinitely good, will give good things to you when you seek them.

I have met with many expositions of this passage in which there is an attempt made to show that the child asked a wrong thing and wanted a stone which seemed to be bread. Nothing of the kind is meant here. The child is not represented as asking for a stone, but as seeking for a proper gift, namely, bread. No mistake at all was made by the child, his prayer was what it should be. And the point of the parable touches the father's answer. The truth taught here is not that God will refuse us evil things if we mistakenly ask for them. That is a truth, but it is not one that is taught here. This verse states that good prayers for good things will be answered, and that they will not be answered by things that just appear to be good, but with the actual good that is desired. I will now try to expand that simple thought.

The three headings are:

1. Right prayers, right answers
2. The best prayer, the surest answer
3. The prayer of the text is best, for it contains all blessings in it.

1. Right prayers, right answers.

First, then, right prayers, right answers. The child asks for bread, his father does not give him a stone; he asks for a fish—there are certain kinds of fish that are very like snakes—but the father does not give him a serpent; the child asks for an egg—we are told by some that certain scorpions when they fold themselves up look like eggs—the father never makes a fool of the child, or injures him by giving him a scorpion for an egg.

If we may be allowed to put some interpretation on this, I should say, if we begin our prayers by asking God for necessities, that is bread, bread temporal, or the bread of life, he will not give us useless, tooth-breaking, unsatisfying stones. We shall have, when we pray for necessary things, the really necessary things themselves—not the imitation of them, but the actual blessings. And if our faith grows a little stronger, after we have received bread we go on to ask for fish, which is not an essential, but a comfort and a delicacy; if we are bold to ask for spiritual comforts, consoling gifts, and enabling graces, something over and above what is absolutely necessary to save us our heavenly Father will not mock us by giving us superficial comforts which might be harmful like serpents. He will give us as much comfort as we can bear, and it will be pure, holy, healthy comfort. And if, becoming more confident still, we ask for an egg, which I take it in Christ's day was a rare luxury, we shall not be deluded by its counterfeit. In only one other place in the Bible, in the Book of Job, do we read about eggs being eaten, and Job was a rich man. All through the Bible we do not find poultry mentioned until our Savior's day. Then, chickens were so valuable that eggs were considered to be the height of luxury, which a child would not be expected to ask for. But if a child was eventually bold enough to ask for this greater favor, his father would not punish him by putting his hand on a deadly scorpion. Even if I can summon up enough faith to ask for the best pleasures and richest graces and the highest Christian blessings, the closest fellowship with Christ, I would not instead receive intoxicating excitement, or delirious fanaticism, or some other deadly thing.

Now, at first sight, this may not appear to be a very useful truth, but I think I can show you that it is. To begin with the common blessings of providence: you have been laying your case before the throne with much earnestness of late, and you have prayed God to guide and lead you in all the steps of life. At this moment you are overwhelmed with trouble, distress has followed distress. Now, do not judge God harshly, above all do not judge him so harshly that you think he is less kind and tender than you are. Your child asking for bread receives bread; you have asked for guidance and you will receive it; you have asked for providential care and you have received it. These present circumstances, which God has given you, are what you have asked for. Your present lot is from the Lord. He has not given you a stone. It seems hard to believe, but it may be the crust of true bread for all that believe it to be so. Never suspect that you are treated ungenerously by your Lord. Were you as able to judge as he is, you would perceive that he has given you what is for your enduring good, and that he has given you the best possible thing. Do not think of your present distress as a stone, a serpent, or a scorpion. If you do this you will be afraid of your mercies and tremble at your consolations. Providential love you have sought and providential love is yours beyond all question, even though trials surround you; for by all these things people live, and in all these is the life of our spirit. God will bring good out of the apparent evil; indeed, if faith will but open her eye it is not apparent evil, but it is even now evidently good.

Blind unbelief misrepresents God's work, while faith's clearer eye discerns the truth. Do not suspect your God of giving you the scorpion instead of the egg. You have asked that here on earth providence may deal wisely with you, and that God may be glorified by you; infinite wisdom is even now fulfilling your hallowed desire; amid fiery trials your faith is honoring God, and every circumstance of your affliction is made subservient to your soul's perfection.

In spiritual matters how often in our earnest anxiety to be right have we questioned whether the spiritual gifts which we have received are what we hope they are, or whether after having sought God's grace we may not after all have missed it. For instance, many of us, I hope most of us, possess today faith in the Lord Jesus Christ; we look to his cross and we are relieved of our load; we see him as our suffering substitute, and our soul feels joy and peace as the result of faith; our faith lays her hand on his head as the scapegoat, and we see sin carried away by him into the wilderness of forgetfulness; but the question will come and sometimes very bitterly, Is this true faith? Is this the faith of God's elect? Is it not after all presumptuous for me to say and believe that in Jesus Christ I am pardoned and saved? There is, evidently, a notional faith; may not mine be that? There is, it seems, a faith of devils, for they "believe and tremble"; may not mine be like that? Is that which I have pleaded with God in prayer for, and which I accepted as my answer, the real grace of faith, or am I after all deluding myself? Look, my brothers and sisters, where did you seek this faith? Did you not ask your heavenly Father to give it you? Have you not devoutly sought, and do you not still seek today, even with tears, that he would work in you the faith which he himself made? Now do you think that he would have given you a stone instead of bread, that he would have put into your heart a worldly desire, or have allowed it to come there while you are waiting for the humble simple faith of God's own people? My Lord, I sought it at thy feet, and there I found it, and it cannot be otherwise than a good and real faith which I found when I looked up to thee. Be assured, O anxious heart, that in the crucial matter of faith, true seekers will not be put off with false faith.

The same question may arise about every spiritual grace. We will look at repentance. I am not for a moment about to depreciate the value of a discriminating doctrine which clearly shows the difference between legal bondage and the evangelical repentance of a child of God, but I suppose few of us can sit under sermons of that kind, especially if the preachers make numerous nice distinctions, without feeling, "I am afraid I come short on several points; I fear that my repentance does not come up to the mark, and I hardly know whether I can quite say that I have so renounced sin, so abhorred it, so detested it, so loathed it from the very bottom of my soul, as this good man describes." Well, then, it will be a sweet thing to fall back on this: I seek repentance from the Holy Spirit through Jesus Christ. I come to my Father and say, "Create in me a new heart, O God. If my heart is not broken and contrite, break it, and heal it if it is." I earnestly desire that the Lord would give me a tender spirit. My longing is towards the repentance which is of his own working. I lay myself down like a field, and ask him to plow me. I put myself before him as the patient places his limb under the surgeon's knife, and I beseech him to deal with me in the most cutting and severe manner just so that he may rid me of the disease of sin. Now, if you sincerely act like this, I am sure you will not be deceived in your repentance; you will receive the repentance that needs not to be repented of. You would not give your child the serpent instead of the fish, neither will God allow you to be deluded with a fake repentance instead of the gospel repentance which is the special watermark of his chosen people.

Now, all our graces may be subjected to the same questioning, and our confidence in them may be reestablished by the same method. If you have sought them from the Lord, and have waited on him in prayer seriously desiring to have whatever he gives, and only what he gives, you will not be deceived or disappointed. The Person from whom you seek these boons is truth itself, and he never mocks his children. If you went to fake mediators and priests, you would be deceived, but you will never be deceived by the one Mediator, Jesus Christ. If you dream that the spiritual boon is to pass through mortal hands, there are priests today like the priests of Egypt, Jannes, and Jambres, who while a fish passes through their hands turn them into serpents, and craftily exchange an egg for a scorpion through a little manipulation. If, then, I received my religion at second hand I may have been deceived, but if I have gone to God himself, my Father, in earnest and importunate prayer, and have desired to receive these blessings direct from his Son and his Spirit, no mistake has taken place. I must have received the good thing I sought.

We will take one more example. My dear brethren, in looking back on all our experience, the doubt will occur to us whether after all it may not have been a fallacy and a delusion. I thought that I was brought out of darkness into God's marvelous light; I thought that I rejoiced in the Lord; I have thought that my prayers had been answered; I have believed that I had been led from grace to grace by his Spirit; I have thought, and if not awfully deceived it is true, that I have had fellowship with the Father and with his Son; I have had but few ecstasies, but I have had much peace; I have had both the mournful and the cheerful experiences of God's people—I think I have; but in dark times we say, "Is it so? Am I after all a true child of God? May I not after all have persuaded myself that I was converted during a revival or under a certain earnest minister? May I not since then have propped up that deceptive supposition by the respect and esteem of Christian people, and may I not up till now have been a deceiver, or self-deceived? May not the whole thing turn out to be one awful sham?" In such a case we come back to this: where did I seek this, and what did I seek? Did I go to God and desire to be a mere professor? Was it my wish to gain a worldly position or to win the respect of my friends by professing to be a Christian, or did I go sincerely to the Lord, and for love of salvation desire to be converted? Did I desire the Savior that I might be reconciled to God, that I might be made holy? And since then have I still desired truly and earnestly to possess the grace which God gives and not the mere imitations of man? Do I pant to have God's own Spirit in my soul, and is that my sincere and earnest prayer now? Well, then, I have no right to suspect that I am deceived. Like a child, I believe that my heavenly Father has given me what I asked for; I have done right in so believing. My child would do me a gross injustice if he suspected that the fish I gave him was not a fish, but a serpent; and I do my God a great injustice if, sincerely knowing that I have sought the one thing needful at his hands through Jesus Christ, I suspected that he has permitted me to be deluded with something else. No, if I sought it from him, and sought it sincerely, I have now the good thing which I longed for.

Now, this simple truth may yet be very, very helpful to you, for nowadays people attack our faith. Some of us have waited on the Lord for teaching, and we have been established in the old faith which people now sneer at as a worn-out creed. We have been taught as we believe, by the Spirit of God, and by God's word; and now because this advanced age and this enlightened century have discovered that these old-fashioned truths are unphilosophical, are we to believe that when we went to God for teaching we did not receive bread, but a stone? I do not believe it, nor will I give up the bread I have long lived on because these men choose to call it a stone. I will hold it still, it is my food, and on it I shall live forever. If a person has sought from God to be filled with zeal until he becomes a burning seraph, some will tell him this is all wild-fire, the person is excited beyond bounds, he ought to be more cool. My dear friends, if you have sought from God the zeal from his house which eats you up, do not believe that the spirit that God has given you is wildfire, that your ardor for the conversion of sinners is fanaticism. Hold on to it and get more of it, and do not let the devil delude you out of the treasure you have gained. The fish is a fish, not a serpent, and the egg is an egg, and not a scorpion. And so, too, when the believer has stood fast in the faith and would not leave it, then he has been told, "It is only your natural obstinacy. You are pig-headed; you have got hold of a thing and there is no making you give it up." Many a godly person has been ridiculed for his determination. "It is not that he has any real martyr's spirit in him, it is only his animal obstinacy." Ah my friend, but know where you got this firmness, and if you wait on the Lord, and say, "Establish me in thy fear, my God; help me to bear accusations from sinners, as my Redeemer did," then God will not give you any evil thing. Having done all still stand, endure to the end, and you will gain the crown of life that never fades.

That is our first point—prayer for good things meets a good answer.

2. The best prayer, the surest answer.

Then, the question arises in every heart: "It seems then that I have only to ascertain that my prayer is for a really good thing, and I shall have it?" Just so, and hence, second, "The prayer for the best thing is surest of an answer," for, says the text,

"How much more shall your heavenly Father give the Holy Spirit to them that ask him?" There is no doubt about the Holy Spirit being a good thing; when we therefore ask for him, for his divine presence and influence, we may rest assured that God will give it. That is the first point under this heading.

(a) God will give the Holy Spirit to those who ask for him

The Holy Spirit is sometimes represented as the wind, the life-giving breath. He blows on the valleys filled up with the slaughtered and they are brought to life. You and I, though we are made to live, often feel that life is flagging, and almost dying. The Spirit of God can bring us to life, revive in us the spark of divine life, and strengthen in our hearts God's life. Pray for this quickening breath, and God will give it to you. As surely as you sincerely pray you will have and feel the revival of the life within.

The Spirit of God is sometimes compared to water. It is he who applies the blood of Jesus and sanctifies us. He cleanses us, fertilizes us. Well, he will come to us in that capacity. Do we feel that our sin has much power over us? O Spirit of God, destroy sin within us and work purity in us. You have already given us the new birth by water and the Spirit, go on and complete your work until our whole nature is formed in the image of the Great First-born. You will have it if you seek it; God will give you this Spirit if you seek for this.

The Holy Spirit is revealed to us under the image of light; he illuminates the mind, he makes our natural darkness flee. Wait upon him, O child of God, that you may be led into all truth. He can make what now perplexes you to become plain; he can enlighten you about truths which are beyond you at the moment. Wait on him! As God's child, long to be taught by God. I do not know how to communicate to you the sense

I feel just now about the deep condescension of God in promising to give us the Holy Spirit. He has given us his Son, and now he promises his Spirit. Here are two gifts, unimaginable in preciousness. Will God dwell with humankind on the earth? Will God dwell in people? Can it be that the infinite Spirit, God over everyone, blessed forever, will dwell in my poor heart and make my body to be his temple? It is certainly so; for as certain as it is that God will give good things to those who ask for good things, he will certainly give the Holy Spirit to those who ask for the Holy Spirit. Sit not in the dark then when God's light will shine on you if you seek it.

The Holy Spirit is described as fire, and in this capacity he kindles enthusiasm of spirit and burning zeal in the hearts of God's people. The tongue of fire speaks with a matchless might; the heart of flame conquers the sons of men. O that we had this fire! It is to be had. The Spirit of God will come in answer to our cries. He will come and fire the church and each individual member of it.

Often the Spirit of God is likened to oil. Through God's Spirit we have the divine anointing. The prayer that the pastor may be anointed with fresh oil is a very welcome one, but it is equally needed that you yourselves have your lamps supplied, that your light may not go out. This desire will be fulfilled. He will give the Holy Spirit in this way to those who ask him for it. As the gentle dropping dew that cheers and refreshes the grass, so the Spirit will come and console our spirits, as they are tired by the heat of this world's busy day. The Holy Spirit will come and fall on us like dew if we seek him. As the blessed dove, bearing peace on his wings, so God's Spirit will come to us. In fact, there is no work of God's Spirit done in us unless we seek it. All of the attributes of God's Spirit can come to us if we ask for them. He will give the Holy Spirit to those who ask him.

(b) It will truly be the Holy Spirit

From the context in which this verse comes I deduce that "it will truly be the Holy Spirit." Go back again to that first thought. The child asks for bread and does not receive a stone; you ask for the Holy Spirit, and you will receive the Holy Spirit. Some people have been misled by an evil spirit. I believe that a great deal of the recent ranting about the date of the second coming of Christ came from an evil spirit. I doubt if there was any humble laying down of minds before God's throne to seek the Holy Spirit. There was probably too much self sufficiency and a great desire for something that would make the person important. This had led many preachers into vain imaginings and fanatical ranting. You will not receive an evil spirit in place of the good Spirit, if you humbly and patiently wait on the Most High. Neither will you be misled by fancy. People will tell you that you are deluded when you experience deep joys, but if you have sincerely and intensely sought the Spirit, then God will give you the Spirit. You do not need to be afraid when you bow before Jehovah's throne in Jesus' name and ask for the Holy Spirit, that you will be sent away with anything other than that Holy Spirit who comes from the Father and the Son.

(c) This Holy Spirit is given in answer to prayer

But it appears clearly enough from the text that "this Holy Spirit is given in answer to prayer." Did we not hear some time ago from certain wise brethren that we were never to pray for the Spirit? I think I heard it often said, "We have the Holy Spirit, and therefore we are not to pray for it." This is similar to that other statement from some of these brethren, that we have pardon for sin, so we are not to pray for pardon for sin, just as if we were never to pray for what we have! If we have life we are to pray that we have it more abundantly. If we have pardon in one respect we are to ask for a fuller appreciation of it; and if we have the Holy Spirit so that we are quickened and saved, we do not ask him in that respect, but we ask for his power in other directions, and for his grace in other forms. I do not go before God now and say, "Lord, I am a dead sinner, quicken me by your Spirit," for I trust I am already alive by his Spirit; but as I am quickened I now cry, "Lord, let not the life you have given me ebb away until it becomes very feeble, but give me your Spirit that the life within me may become strong and mighty, and may subdue all the power of death within my members, that I may be strong and vigorous as a result of your Spirit." O you who have the Spirit, you are the very people to pray that you may experience more of his matchless work and gracious influences, and through his indwelling may seek to know him better and better. Be encouraged by this: God will give the Holy Spirit to those who ask him. Ever since certain brethren gave up asking for the Holy Spirit they have not had it, and they have wandered into many errors. If they will not ask they will not have, but may we wait humbly and patiently on the Lord that he may daily give us his Spirit.

(d) Know how to give

I desire earnestly to call your attention to one thing which our Savior says: "If ye being evil *know how to give* good gifts unto your children," how ought the sentence to be completed? "how much more shall your heavenly Father *know how to give* the Holy Spirit to them that ask him?" Is that not the right way to complete the sentence? Of course it is, but Jesus does not say that. He very kindly puts it, in the first place, that we "know how to give good gifts," for sometimes we know how to give them, but we cannot do it. It is a bitter thing, and yet it has sometimes happened that the child has said, "Father, give me bread" and with a breaking heart the father has had to reply, "My child, there is none." It must be one of the hardest human trials, and yet it is the trial that tens of thousands of people in this city have to endure, as they say, "No, there is not even a crust of bread for my child." You see the father knows how, but he cannot do it. But the text does not say that God knows how to give the Holy Spirit, it says a great deal more than that, it declares that he does give, because with him to know how is the same thing as to do it. He gives the Holy Spirit to those who ask him. He does not only know how, but he does it. Never does he have to say to his child, "My child, I cannot." The poor sinner says, "Lord, help me to repent," and the Lord never says, "I have not enough of the Holy Spirit for that." Boundlessly will he give if faith only dares to open her mouth wide. You are not straitened in him; you are straitened in yourselves.

I am not telling you anything new, but a very simple truth, and yet for all that a truth which we do not put into practice. We may have the Spirit of God resting on us. As Stephen was a person filled with the Holy Spirit, even so may we be. We seek all the spiritual uplifting which the Holy Spirit gave to people of old, and he can give it to us still. Though he will not reveal new truths—for we do not ask this from him, as we already have the complete gospel revealed—he will bring home the old truths to our souls and make them potent in our consciences, in our lives, and this is what we want. If you are only just Christians, and are not glorifying God, nor living near him, nor mighty in prayer, nor well taught in Scripture, nor useful in your lives; I beseech you to remember, if you do not have the Spirit it is because you do not seek him importunately, and do not seek him with a deep sense of your need of him. If you, being evil, give your children bread, how much more will God give you the Spirit; and as you, being evil, do not mock your child by putting him off without bread, and giving him something else, neither will your heavenly Father. He will give you the real Spirit; his own gentle, truthful, infallible, Holy Spirit he will give to those who ask him.

3. The best of prayers, which is sure to be heard, is also a most comprehensive one.

From the parallel passage in Matthew (Mt 7:11) note that Matthew says nothing about the egg, but says, "If ye then, being evil, know how to give good gifts unto your children, how much more shall your Father which is in heaven give *good things* to them that ask him?" Now what does our text say? "How much more shall your heavenly Father give *the Holy Spirit* to them that ask him?" Is it not clear then that the Holy Spirit is the equivalent to "good things," and that in fact when the Lord gives us the Holy Spirit he gives us all "good things"? What a comprehensive prayer then is the prayer for the Spirit of God! Sit down with a pencil and blank sheet of paper and write down all your spiritual needs. I will see how wise you are by the length of the list, for if you know yourself you will find you do not already possess everything, and you are a great mass of need. To pray for all these things separately may seem to be a very long exercise. But just take the pencil and do as a school child does with an addition sum, and see what the total adds up to. You will find it comes to this: the Holy Spirit. "My God, give me your Holy Spirit, and I have all." "But do we not need the Savior?" asks someone. Yes that is true, but the Holy Spirit when he comes "takes the things of Christ and shows them to us." That is the greatest value of the Holy Spirit. "He shall glorify me." Wherever the Spirit of God comes there comes the blood of the atonement, we are brought close by it, and every spiritual blessing bought with blood is brought home to the soul by the Holy Spirit. If you have the Spirit he does not come empty-handed. He comes loaded with all the treasures of the covenant, the blessings ordained for you from before the foundation of the world, and the blessings given to you in the covenant of grace, and the blessings bought for you by Jesus' precious blood. Do, then, let this be your prayer: "Give me, O God, your Holy Spirit!"

Then your prayer is intercessory as well as for yourselves. You pray for your children, for your wife, for your neighbors, for your friends. I hope your intercessory roll is a long one. If God gives you power to bless people by your prayers, do not cramp the blessing. What is it that you want for others? In one word, it is the Holy Spirit. Let the Holy Spirit be given to that dear son of yours, and he will have a tender conscience—you have often wished he had; he will have a desire to follow after Christ, and he will find Christ; he will be a Christian. Let the Holy Spirit be given to that dear daughter of yours. She will have a desire for the word of God, a love for the means of grace; she will find the Savior, she will become a useful Christian woman. Your neighbors, you prayed that they might go with you to hear the gospel, and a very excellent prayer it was. Still it would be a fuller prayer that the Spirit would visit them. Some have been visited by the Holy Spirit who have not been in the house of God. Even at their work divine impulses they could not account for have followed them. The fact is, the hearing of the word is but the vehicle, the power lies in the Spirit of God. I put it to you, therefore, whether it is not a most fitting prayer for you to offer for your neighbors and family?

Tomorrow is a day of prayer. I hope you may all with one accord be in one place in prayer. But I humbly suggest that we should all pray throughout the day and beyond, that God will give to his churches more and more of the Holy Spirit. I believe that the heart of England is honeycombed with a detestable infidelity, which dares still to go into the pulpit, and call itself Christian. My prayer shall go up that God will give us the Holy Spirit, for people never go wrong with the Holy Spirit. He keeps them right and leads them into all truth. Soundness of teaching is only worth having when it is the result of the living indwelling of God in the church; and because too much of the Holy Spirit has departed, we see the signs that the orthodox faith is given up, and the inventions of man preached instead.

Sometimes I breathe this prayer as I walk along: that God would raise up more ministers to preach the gospel with power; there is so much feeble preaching, mere twaddling, and so little declaration of the gospel with power. But I do not know that I will pray that prayer again; I will pray this one: "Lord, send your Spirit upon the churches!" Then the right preachers and faithful laborers will come. The Spirit of God will touch their tongues with fire, and they will say, "Here am I, send me." The Spirit of God is the power of the church, and speaks with might in her.

My longing is that the churches may be more holy. I grieve to see so much worldly conformity; how often wealth leads men astray; how many Christians follow the fashions of this wicked world. But shall I pray that the churches may be holy? I will, but I will put my prayer in this form: I will ask that God will give the Holy Spirit. He is the Spirit of holiness, he leads to obedience, purges from sin and creates the image of God in his people.

I desire to see more unity among the churches. It is a pity when churches fall out, and chide, and fight. Ecclesiastical quarrels are generally more bitter than any other. Do not just pray for unity, but rather pray, "Lord, give the Holy Spirit." For if the Holy Spirit is in us and abounds in us we shall not be divided—the church of God will feel the unity among God's people. We must plead in prayer with our Father, who did not spare his own Son, but freely gave him for us all, who will also freely give us all things, if we know how to ask aright.

PART 3

The Key to
Revival

CHAPTER NINE

The Key to Revival

*Nevertheless I have somewhat against thee,
because thou hast left thy first love. Remember
therefore from whence thou art fallen, and
repent, and do the first works; or else I will
come unto thee quickly, and will remove thy
candlestick out of his place, except thou repent.*
REVELATION 2:4-5

It was the work of the priest to go into the holy place and to
trim the seven-branched lamp of gold: see how our High
Priest walks in the middle of the seven golden candlesticks: his
work is not occasional, but constant. Wearing robes which are
at once royal and priestly, he is seen lighting the holy lamps,
pouring in the sacred oil, and removing impurities which
would dim the light.

(a) The constant worker
Hence our Lord's fitness to deal with the churches which are
the golden lampstands, for no one knows so much about the
lamps as the person whose constant work it is to watch them

and trim them. No one knows the churches as Jesus does, for the care of all the churches daily comes on him, he continually walks among them, and holds their ministers as stars in his right hand. His eyes are perpetually on the churches, so that he knows their deeds, their sufferings, and their sins; and those eyes are like a flame of fire, so that he sees with penetration, discernment, and accuracy which nobody else can reach. We sometimes judge the condition of religion too leniently, or else we err on the other side and judge too severely. Our eyes are dim with the world's smoke; but his eyes are like a flame of fire. He sees the churches through and through, and knows their true condition much better than they know themselves. The Lord Jesus Christ is a most careful observer of churches and individuals; nothing is hidden from his observant eye.

(b) The careful observer

As he is the most careful observer, so he is the most candid. He is always "the faithful and true witness." He loves much, and therefore he never judges harshly. He loves much, and therefore he always judges jealously. Jealousy is the sure attendant of such love as his. He will neither speak smooth words nor bitter words; but he will speak the truth—the truth in love, the truth as he himself perceives it, and as he would have us perceive it. Well may he say, "He that hath an ear, let him hear what the Spirit saith unto the churches," since his sayings are so true, so just, so weighty.

(c) The tender observer

Certainly no observer can be so tender as the Son of God. Those lamps are very precious to him: it cost him his life to light them. "Christ loved the church, and gave himself for it." Every church is to our Lord a more sublime thing than a constellation in the heavens: as he is precious to his saints, so are they precious to him. He cares little about empires, kingdoms, or republics; but his heart is set on the kingdom of righteousness, of which his cross is the royal standard. He must reign until his foes are vanquished, and this is the great thought on his mind here: "from henceforth expecting till his enemies be made his footstool." He never ceases to watch over his church: his sacrifice has ended, but not his service in caring for the golden lamps. He has completed the redemption of his bride, but he continues her preservation.

Therefore, I feel at this time that we may well join in a prayer to our Lord Jesus to come into our midst and put our light in order. Oh for a visit from himself such as he paid in vision to the seven churches of Asia! With him is the oil to feed the living flame, and he knows how to pour in the correct measure. With him are those golden snuffers with which to remove every superfluity of naughtiness, that our lights may so shine before men that they may see our good works and glorify our Father who is in heaven. Oh for his presence now, to search us and to sanctify us; to make us shine forth to his Father's praise. We would be judged by the Lord, that we may not be condemned with the world. We would pray this morning, "Search my thoughts; and see if there be any wicked way in me, and lead me in the way everlasting." All things are naked and open to the eyes of him with whom we have to do; and we delight to have it so. We invite thee, O great High Priest, to come into this thy sanctuary, and look to this thy lamp this morning.

In the text, as it is addressed to the church at Ephesus and to us, we note three things. First, we note that Christ perceives: "I know thy works… nevertheless I have somewhat against thee." Second, Christ prescribes: "Remember, therefore, from whence thou art fallen, and repent." Third, Christ persuades—

persuades with a threatening: "I will remove thy candlestick out of his place"; persuades also, with a promise: "To him that overcometh will I give to eat of the tree of life, which is in the midst of the Paradise of God." If the Lord himself is here at this time, our plan of discourse will be a river of life; but if he is not among us by his Holy Spirit, it will be as the dry bed of a torrent which bears the name of "river," but lacks the living stream. We expect our Lord's presence; he will come to the lamps which his office calls on to trim; it has been his way to be with us; some of us have met him this morning already, and we have constrained him to tarry with us.

1. Christ perceives.

First, then, we notice that he perceives. Our Lord sorrowfully perceives the faults of his church—"Nevertheless I have somewhat against thee"; but he does not so look at these faults to miss what is admirable in the church. For he begins his letter with commendations. "I know thy works, and thy labor, and thy patience, and how thou canst not bear them which are evil." Do not think, my brethren, that our Beloved is blind to the beauties of his church. On the contrary, he delights to observe them. He can see the beauties where she herself cannot see them. Where we observe much to deplore, his loving eyes see much to admire. The graces which he himself creates he can always perceive. When we overlook them in the earnestness of self-examination, and write bitter things against ourselves, the Lord Jesus sees even in those bitter self-condemnations a life and earnestness and sincerity which he loves. Our Lord has a keen eye for all that is good. When he searches our hearts he never passes by the faintest longing, or desire, or faith, or love, of any of his people. He says, "I know thy works."

But this is our point at this time, that while Jesus can see all that is good, yet in staying faithful he sees all that is evil. His love is not blind. He does not say, "As many as I love I commend"; but, "As many as I love, I rebuke and chasten." It is more important for us that we should discover our faults than that we should dwell on our virtues. So notice in this text that Christ perceives the flaw in this church, even in the middle of her earnest service. The church at Ephesus was full of work. "I know thy works and thy labor, and for my name's sake thou hast labored, and hast not fainted." It was such a hardworking church that it pushed on and on with diligent perseverance, and never seemed to flag in its divine mission. Oh that we could say as much about all our churches! I have lived to see many brilliant projects started and left half-finished. I have heard about schemes which were to illuminate the world, but not a spark remains. Holy perseverance is greatly to be desired. During these past thirty-three years we thank God that he has enabled us to labor and not to faint. There has been a continuance of everything attempted, and no drawing back from anything. "This is the work, this is the labor," to hold out even to the end.

Oh how I have dreaded lest we should have to give up any holy enterprise or cut short any gracious effort. Hitherto has the Lord helped us. With people and means, liberality and zeal, he has supplied us. In this case the angel of the church has been very little of an angel from heaven, but very much a human angel; for in the weakness of my flesh and in the heaviness of my spirit have I pursued my calling; but I have pursued it. By God's help I continue to this day, and this church with equal footsteps is at my side; for which the whole praise is due to the Lord, who does not grow tired or become weary. Having put my hand to the plow I have not looked back, but have steadily pressed forward, making straight furrows; but it has been by the grace of God alone.

Alas! Under all the laboring the Lord Jesus perceived that the Ephesians had left their first love; and this was a very serious fault. So it may be in this church; every wheel may continue to revolve, and the whole machinery of ministry may be kept going at its normal rate, and yet there may be a great secret evil which Jesus perceives, and this may be marring everything.

But this church at Ephesus was not only hardworking, it was patient in suffering and underwent great persecution. Christ says of it, "I know your works and your patience, and how thou hast borne, and hast patience, and hast not fainted." Persecution upon persecution visited the faithful, but they bore it all with holy courage and constancy, and continued still confessing their Lord. This was good, and the Lord highly approved it; but yet underneath it he saw the tokens of decline; they had left their first love. So there may seem to be all the patient endurance and dauntless courage that there should be, and yet as a fair apple may have a worm at its core, so may it be with the church when it looks best to the eye of friends.

The Ephesian church excelled in something else, namely, its discipline, its soundness in the faith, and faithfulness towards heretics; for the Lord says of it, "How canst thou not bear them which are evil." They would not have it: they would not tolerate false doctrine, they would not put up with unclean living. They fought against evil, not only in the common people, but in prominent individuals. "Thou hast tried them which say they are apostles, and are not, and hast found them liars." They have dealt with the great ones; they had not flinched from the unmasking of falsehood. Those who seemed to be apostles they had dragged to the light and discovered to be deceivers.

This church was not honeycombed with doubt; it laid no claim to breadth of thought and liberality of view; it was honest to its Lord. He says of it, "This thou hast, thou hatest the deeds of the Nicolaitans, which I also hate." This was to their credit, as it showed a backbone of truth. I wish some of the churches of this age had a little of this holy decision about them; for nowadays, if a person is clever, he may preach the vilest lie that was ever vomited from the mouth of hell, and it will go down with some. He may assail every doctrine of the gospel, he may blaspheme the Holy Trinity, he may trample on the blood of the Son of God, and yet nothing is said about it if he is held in high esteem as a man of advanced thinking and liberal ideas. The church at Ephesus was not of this mind. She was strong in her convictions; she could not yield the faith, nor play the traitor to her Lord. For this her Lord commended her: and yet he says, "I have somewhat against thee, because thou hast left thy first love." When love dies orthodox doctrine becomes a corpse, a powerless formalism. Adhesion to the truth sours into bigotry when the sweetness and light of love to Jesus depart. Love Jesus, and then it is well to hate the deeds of the Nicolaitans; but mere hatred of evil will tend towards evil if love of Jesus is not there to sanctify it. I need not make a personal application; but what is spoken to Ephesus may be spoken at this hour to ourselves. As we hope that we may appropriate the commendation, so let us see whether the expostulation may not also apply to us. "I have somewhat against thee, because thou hast left thy first love." Thus I have shown you that Jesus sees the evil beneath all the good: he does not ignore the good, but he will not pass over the ill.

So, next, this evil was a very serious one. It was love in decline: "thou hast left thy first love." "Is that serious?" asks someone. It is the most serious illness of all; for the church is the bride of Christ, and for a bride to fail in love is to fail in all things. It is idle for the wife to say that she is obedient, and so forth; if love for her husband has evaporated, her wifely duty cannot be fulfilled, she has lost the very life and soul of the marriage state. So, my brethren, this is a most important matter, our love for Christ, because it touches the very heart of the communion with him which is the crown and essence of our spiritual life. As a church we must love Jesus, or else we have lost our reason for existence. A church has not reason for being a church when she has no love within her heart or when that love grows cold. Have I not reminded you that almost any disease may be hopefully endured except the disease of the heart? So when our sickness is heart disease, it is full of danger; and it was so in this case. "Thou hast left thy first love." It is a disease of the heart, a central, fatal disease, unless the great Physician intervenes and delivers us from it. Oh, in any man, in any woman, in any child of God here, let alone in the church as a whole, if there is a leaving of the first love, it is a woeful thing! Lord, have mercy upon us: Christ, have mercy upon us: this should be our solemn litany at once. No peril can be greater than this. Lose love, lose all. Leave out first love, and we have left strength, and peace, and joy, and holiness.

I call your attention, however, to this point, that it was Christ who found it out. "I have somewhat against thee, because thou hast left thy first love." Jesus himself found it out! I do not know how it strikes you; but as I thought it over this fact brought tears to my eyes. When I begin to stop loving Christ or love him less than I should, I would like to find it out myself; and if I did so, there would soon be a cure for it. But for him to find it out, oh, it seems so hard, so sad a thing! That we should keep on growing cold, and cold, and cold, and never care about it until the Beloved points it out to us. Why, even the angel of the church did not find it out; the minister did not know it; but he saw it who loves us so well, that he delights in our love, and pines when it begins to fail. To him we are unutterably dear; he loved us up out of the pit into his heart, loved us up from the dunghill among beggars to sit at his right hand upon his throne; and it is sorrowful that he should have to complain about our cooling love while we are utterly indifferent to the matter. Does Jesus care more about our love than we do? He loves us better than we love ourselves. How good of him to care one jot about our love! This is no complaint of an enemy, but of a dear wounded friend.

I notice that Jesus found it out with great pain. I can hardly conceive a greater grief to him as the husband of his church than to look her in the face and say, "Thou hast left thy first love." What can she give him but love? Will she deny him this? A poor thing is the church left to herself: her Lord married her when she was a beggar; and if she does not give him love, what has she to give him? If she begins to be unfaithful in heart to him, what is she worth? Why, an unloving wife is a foul fountain of discomfort and dishonor to her husband. O beloved, shall it be so with thee? Will you grieve Emmanuel? Will you wound your Well-Beloved? Church of God, will you grieve him whose heart was pierced for your redemption? Brother, sister, can you and I let Jesus find out that our love is departing, that we are ceasing to be zealous for his name? Can we wound him so? Is not this to crucify the Lord afresh? Might he not hold up his hands this morning with fresh blood on them, and say, "These are the wounds which I received in the house of my friends. It was nothing that I died for them, but it is not terrible that, after having died for them, they have failed to give me their hearts?" Jesus is not so sick of our sin as of our lukewarmness. It is a sad business to my heart; I hope it will be sad to all whom it concerns, that our Lord should be the first to spy out our declines in love.

The Savior, having thus seen this with pain, now points it out! As I read this passage over to myself, I noticed that the Savior had nothing to say about the sins of the heathen among whom the Ephesians lived. They are alluded to because it must have been the heathen who persecuted the church, and caused it to endure, and exhibit patience. The Savior, however, has nothing to say against the heathen; and he does not say much more than a word about those who are evil. These had been thrown out. He merely says: "Thou canst not bear them which are evil." He denounced no judgment upon the Nicolaitans, except that he hated them; and even the apostles who were found to be liars, the Master dismisses with that word. He leaves the ungodly in their own condemnation. But what he has to say against his own beloved: "I have somewhat to say against thee." It seems as if the Master might pass over sin in a thousand others, but he cannot wink at failure of love in his own married one. "The Lord thy God is a jealous God." The Savior loves, so that his love is cruel as the grave against coldheartedness. He said of the church of Laodicea, "I will spew thee out of my mouth." This was one of his own churches, too, and yet she made him sick with her lukewarmness. God grant that we may not be guilty of such a crime as that!

The Savior pointed out the failure of love; and when he pointed it out he called it by a lamentable name. "Remember therefore from whence thou art fallen." He calls it a fall to leave our first love. Brothers, sisters, this church had not been licentious, it had not gone over to false doctrines, it had not become idle, it had not been cowardly in the hour of persecution; but this one sin summed up the whole—she did not love Christ as she once loved him, and he calls this a fall. A fall indeed it is. "Oh, I thought," someone says, "that if a member of the church gets drunk that would be a worse fall." That is wrong. But it is a fall if we become intoxicated with the world and lose the freshness of our devotion to Jesus. It is a fall from a high estate of fellowship to the dust of worldliness. "Thou art fallen." The word sounds very harsh in my ears—no, not harsh, for his love speaks it. But it thunders deep down in my soul. I cannot bear it. It is so sadly true. "Thou art fallen." "Remember from whence thou art fallen." Indeed, O Lord, we have fallen when we have left our first love for thee.

The Master evidently counts this decline of love to be a personal wrong done to himself. "I have somewhat against thee." It is not an offense against the king, nor against the judge, but against the Lord Jesus as the husband of the church: an offense against the very heart of Christ himself. "I have somewhat against thee." He does not say, "Thy neighbor has something against thee, thy God has something against thee," but "I, I thy hope, thy joy, thy delight, thy Savior, I have this against thee." The word "somewhat" is an intruder here. Our translators put it in italics, and well they might, for it is a bad word, since it seems to make a small thing of a very grave charge. The Lord has this against us, and it is no mere "somewhat." Come, brothers and sisters, if we have not broken any law, nor offended in any way in grieving another person, this is sorrow enough, if our love has grown in the least degree chill towards Christ; for we have done a terrible wrong to our best friend. This is the bitterness of our offense: Against thee, thee only, have I sinned, and done this evil in thy sight, that I have left my first love. The Savior tells us this most lovingly. I wish I knew how to speak as tenderly as he does; and yet I feel at this moment that I can and must be tender in this matter, for I am speaking about myself as much as about anybody else. I am grieving, grieving over some who are present this morning, grieving for all of us, but grieving most of all for myself, that our Well-Beloved should have reason to say, "I have somewhat against thee, because thou hast left thy first love."

So much for what our Lord perceives. Holy Spirit, bless it to us!

2. Christ prescribes.

And now, second, let us note what the Savior prescribes. The Savior's prescription is couched in these three words: "Remember," "Repent," "Return."

(a) Remember

"Thou hast left thy first love." Remember, then, what thy first love was, and compare your present condition with it. At first nothing diverted you from your Lord. He was your life, your love, your joy. Now you look for recreation somewhere else, and other charms and other beauties win your heart. Are you not ashamed of this? Once you were never tired with hearing about Christ and his gospel: many sermons, many prayer-meetings, many Bible readings, and yet none too many. Now sermons are long, and services are dull, and you must have your jaded appetite excited with novelties. How is this? Once you were never displeased with Jesus whatever he did with you. If you had been sick, or poor, or dying, you would still have loved and blessed his name for all things. He remembers this fondness, and regrets its departure. He says to you today, "I remember you, the kindness of your youth, your love when you searched after me in the wilderness." You would have gone anywhere after your Lord in those days: across the sea, or through the fire, you would have pursued him; nothing would have been too hot or too heavy for you then. Is it so now? Remember! Remember from what you have fallen. Remember the vows, the tears, the communions, the happy days; remember and compare them with your present state.

Remember and consider, that when you were in your first love, that love was not so warm. Even then, when you did live to Christ, and for Christ, and with Christ, you were not so holy, not so consecrated, not so zealous. If you were not so advanced then, think about how you are now—now that you have come down even from that poor attainment. Remember the past with sad forebodings of the future. If you had come down from where you were, who is to tell you where you will end up falling to? He who has sunk so far may fall much further. Is it not so? Though you say in your heart, like Hazael, "Is thy servant a dog?" you may turn out worse than a dog. You may prove to be a wolf! Who knows? You may even now be a devil! You may turn out to be a Judas, a son of perdition, and deny your Master, selling him for thirty pieces of silver. When a stone begins to fall it falls with an ever-increasing rate; and when a soul begins to leave its first love, it quits it more and more, and more and more, until at last it falls terribly. Remember!

(b) Repent

The next word in the prescription is "Repent." Repent as you did at first. The word so appropriate to sinners is appropriate for you, for you have grievously sinned. Repent of the wrong you have done your Lord by leaving your first love for him. If you could lead the life of a seraph, only breathing Christ's love, only existing for him, you would have done little enough. But to leave your first love, how grievously you have wronged him. That love was well-deserved, was it not? Why, then, have you left it? Is Jesus less fair than he was? Does he love thee less than he did? Has he been less kind and tender to you than he used to be? Say, have you outgrown him? Can you do without him? Have you a hope of salvation apart from him? I challenge you, repent of this evil towards One who has greater claim on your love than he ever had. He ought to be loved today more than you ever loved him at your best. O my heart, is not all this most certainly true? How badly you are behaving! How ungrateful you are. Repent! Repent!

Repent of much good which you have left undone through lack of love. Oh, if you had always loved your Lord at your best, what you might have known about him by now. What good deeds you might have done through the power of his love. How many hearts you might have won for your Lord if your own heart had been fuller of love, if your own soul had been more on fire! You have lived the life of a poor beggar because you have allowed such a poverty of love to take you over.

Repent! Repent! To my mind, as I thought over the text, the call for repentance grew louder and louder, because of the occasion of its utterance. Here is the gracious Lord, coming to his church and speaking to her angel in tones of tender kindness. He condescends to visit his people in all his majesty and glory, intending nothing but to manifest himself in love to his own elect as he does not to the world. And yet he is compelled even then to give a chiding, and to say, "I have this against thee, because thou hast left thy first love." Here is a love visit clouded with a telling off—a necessary telling off. What a mischief sin has done. It is a dreadful thing that when Jesus comes to his own dear bride he should have to speak in grief and not in joy. Must holy communion, which is the wine of heaven, be embittered with the tonic of expostulation? I see the upper springs of close fellowship, where the waters of life leap from their first source in the heart of God. Are not these streams most pure and precious? If a person drinks from this he will live forever. Shall it be that even at the fountainhead they will be dashed with bitterness? Even when Christ communes personally with us must he say, "I have somewhat against thee"? Break, my heart, that it should be so! Well may we repent with a deep repentance when our greatest joys are flavored with the bitter herbs of regret, that our best Beloved should have something against us.

(c) Return

But then he says in effect, "Return." The third word is this— "Repent, and do the first works." Notice that he does not say, "Repent, and get back thy first love." This seems rather strange. But then love is the chief of the first deeds, and, moreover, the first deeds can only come from the first love. There must be in every declining Christian a practical repentance. Do not be satisfied with regrets and resolves. Do the first deeds; do not strain after the first emotions, but do the first deeds. No renewal is so valuable as the practical cleansing of our way. If the life is made right, it will prove that the love is so. In doing the first deeds you will prove that you have come back to your first love.

The prescription is complete, because the doing of the first works is meant to include the feeling of the first feelings, the sighing of the first sighs, the enjoying of the first joys: these are all supposed to accompany returning obedience and activity.

We are to return to these first deeds at once. Most people come to Christ with a leap; and I have observed that many who come back to him usually do so at a bound. The slow revival of one's love is almost an impossibility; as well expect the dead to be risen by degrees. Love for Christ is often love at first sight! We see him and are conquered by him. If we grow cold the best thing we can do is to fix our eyes on him until we cry, "My soul melted while my Beloved spake." It is a happy circumstance if I can cry, "Or ever I was aware, my soul made me like the chariots of Amminadib." How sweet for the Lord to put us back again at once into the old place, back again in a moment! My prayer is that it may be so this morning with any declining person. May you so repent as not merely to feel the old feelings, but instantly to do the first deeds, and be once more as eager, as zealous, as generous, as prayerful, as you used to be. If we should again see you breaking the alabaster box, we should know that the old love had returned. May the good Master help us to do as well as ever, yes, much better than before!

Notice, however, that this will require a great deal of effort and warfare; for the promise which is made is "to him that overcometh." Overcoming implies conflict. Depend on it, if you conquer a wandering heart, you will have to fight for it. "To him that overcometh," he says, "will I give to eat of the tree of life." You must fight your way back to the garden of the Lord. You will have to fight against lethargy, against an evil heart of unbelief, against the numbing influence of the world. In the name and power of him who bids you repent, you must wrestle and struggle until you achieve the mastery over self and yield your whole nature to your Lord.

So I have shown you how Christ prescribes. Now I wish to dwell with earnestness on the last part. I have no desire to say a word by which I should show myself off as an orator, but I long to speak a word by which I may prove myself a true brother pleading with you in deep sympathy, because in all the ill which I rebuke I mourn my own personal share. Bless us, O Spirit of the Lord!

3. Christ persuades.

Now see, brethren, Christ persuades. This is the third point: the Lord Jesus persuades his erring one to repent.

First, he persuades with a warning: "I will come unto thee"; "quickly" is not in the original: the Revised Version has left it out. Our Lord is generally very slow at the work of judgment: "I will come unto thee, and will remove thy candlestick out of its place, except thou repent." This he must do: he cannot allow his light to be apart from his love, and if the first love is left, the church shall be left in darkness. The truth must always shine, but not always in the same place. The place must be made fit by love or the light will be removed.

Our Lord means, first, I will take away the comfort of the word. He raises up certain ministers, and makes them burning and shining lights in the middle of his church, and when the people gather together they are cheered and enlightened by their shining. A ministry blessed by the Lord is a singular comfort to God's church. The Lord can easily take away that light which has brought comfort to so many: he can remove the good man to another sphere or he can call him home to his rest. Death can put out the candle which now gladdens the house. The church which has lost a ministry by which the Lord's glory has shone forth has lost a good deal; and if this loss has been sent in chastisement for decline of love it is all the harder to bear. I can point you to places where once there was a man of God, and all went well; but the people grew cold, and the Lord took away their leader, and the place is now a desolation. Those who now attend those courts and listen to a modern ministry cry out because of the famine of the word of the Lord. O friends, let us value the light while we have it and prove that we do so by benefiting from it; but how can we profit if we leave our first love? The Lord may take away our comfort as a church if our first zeal dies down.

But the candlestick also symbolizes usefulness: it is by which a church shines. The use of a church is to preserve the truth, wherewith to illuminate the neighborhood, to illuminate the world. God can soon cut short our usefulness, and he will do so if we cut short our love. If the Lord is withdrawn, we can go on with our work as we used to do, but nothing will come of it: we can go on with Sunday schools, mission stations, branch churches, and yet accomplish nothing. Brethren, we can go on with the Orphanage, the College, the Colportage, the Evangelistic Society, the Book Fund, and everything else, and yet nothing will be effected if the arm of the Lord is not made bare.

He can, if he wills, take away from the church her very existence as a church. Ephesus is gone: nothing but ruins can be found. The Lord can soon take away our candlesticks out of their places if the church uses her light for her own glory and is not filled with his love. God forbid that we should fall under this condemnation. Of thy mercy, O Lord, forbid it! Let it not so happen to any of us. Yet this may occur to us as individuals. You, dear brother or sister, if you lose your first love, may soon lose your joy, your peace, your usefulness. You, who are now so bright, may grow dull. You, who are now so useful, may become useless. You were once an instructor of the foolish, and a teacher of babes; but if the Lord is withdrawn you will instruct nobody, you will be in the dark yourself. Alas, you may come to lose the very name of Christian, as some have done who once seemed to be burning and shining lights. They were foolish virgins, and before long they were heard to cry, "Our lamps are gone out!" The Lord can and will take away the candlestick out of its place if we put him out of his place by a failure in our love for him.

How can I persuade you better than with the warning words of my Master? My beloved, I persuade you from my very soul not to encounter these dangers, not to run these terrible risks; for as you would not wish to see either the church or your own self without God's light, to pine in darkness, it is necessary that you abide in Christ and go on to love him more and more.

The Savior holds out a promise as his other way of persuading. It seems a very wonderful promise to me: "To him that overcometh will I give to eat of the tree of life, which is in the midst of the paradise of God." Observe, those who lose their first love fall, but those who abide in love are made to stand. In contrast with the fall which took place in God's paradise, we have man eating from the tree of life, and so living forever. If we, through grace, overcome the common tendency to decline in love, then we will be confirmed and settled in the Lord's favor. By eating from the tree of knowledge of good and evil we fell; by eating from the fruit of a better tree we live and stand fast forever. Life proved true by love shall be nourished on the best of food; it shall be sustained by the fruit from the garden of the Lord himself, gathered by the Savior's own hand.

Note again, those who lose their first love wander far, they depart from God. "But," says the Lord, "if you keep your first love you shall not wander, but you shall come into closer fellowship. I will bring you nearer to the center. I will bring you to eat from the tree of life which is in the middle of God's paradise." The inner ring is for those who grow in love; the center of all joy is only to be reached by much love. We know

God as we love God. We enter into his paradise as we abide in his love. What joy is here! What a reward love has!

Then notice the mystical blessing which lies here, waiting for your meditation. Do you know how we fell? The woman took the fruit from the forbidden tree and gave it to Adam, and Adam ate and fell. The reverse is the case in the promise in front of us: the Second Adam takes the divine fruit from the tree of promise and hands it to his wife; she eats and lives forever. He who is the Father of the age of grace hands down to us immortal joys, which he has plucked from an undying tree. The reward of love is to eat the fruit of life. "We are getting into mysteries," someone says. Yes, I am intentionally lifting a corner of the veil, and no more. I only mean to give you a glimpse at the promised boon. Into his innermost joys our Lord will bring us if we keep up our first love and go from strength to strength therein. Marvelous things are locked up in the caskets whereof love holds the key. Sin set the angel with a flaming sword between us and the tree of life in the middle of the garden; but love has quenched that sword, and now the angels beckon us to come into the innermost secrets of paradise. We shall know as we are known when we love as we are loved. We shall live the life of God when we are wholly taken up with the love of God. The love of Jesus answered by our love for Jesus makes the sweetest music the heart can know. No joy on earth is equal to the bliss of being completely taken up with loving Christ. If I had my choice of all the lives that I could live, I certainly would not choose to be an emperor, nor a millionaire, nor a philosopher; for power, and wealth, and knowledge bring with them sorrow and travail; but I would choose to have nothing to do but to love my Lord Jesus—nothing, I mean, but to do all things for his sake, and out of love for him. Then I know that I should be in paradise, yes, in the middle of the paradise of God, and I should have meat to eat which is all unknown to the people of the world.

Heaven on earth is abounding love towards Jesus. This is the first and last of true delight—to love him who is the first and the last. To love Jesus is another name for paradise. Lord, let me know this by continual experience. "You are soaring aloft," cries one. Yes, I own it. Oh, that I could allure you to a heavenward flight upon the wings of love! There is a bitterness in declining love: it is a very consumption of the soul, and makes us weak, and faint, and low. But true love is the foretaste of glory. See the heights, the glittering heights, the glorious heights, the everlasting hills to which the Lord of life will conduct all those who are faithful to him through the power of his Holy Spirit. See, O love, thine ultimate abode. I pray that what I have said may be blessed by the Holy Spirit so we all are brought closer to the Bridegroom of our souls. Amen.